BASEMENT WOMEN

LUTHERAN CHURCH BASEMENT WOMEN

BY
JANET LETNES MARTIN
and ALLEN TODNEM

Illustrated by
ALLEN TODNEM

REDBIRD PRODUCTIONS
BOX 274
HASTINGS, MN 55033

Printed in the United States of America

Published by: Redbird Productions
Box 274
Hastings, MN 55033

ISBN 10: 1-88627-16-9
ISBN 13: 978-1-88627-169-2

SECOND EDITION
Editor: Linda Lewis
Contributing Editor: Suzann Nelson
Illustrated by: Allen Todnem
Cover Design: Beth Vandewalker
Printer: Sentinel Printing, St. Cloud, MN

WWW.SCANDINAVIANMARKET.COM

LUTHERAN CHURCH BASEMENT WOMEN
Table of Contents

THIS BOOK IS DEDICATED
TO LUTHERAN CHURCH BASEMENT WOMEN

LUTHERAN SONG, POEM & PRAYER

Verse 2

Sometimes it is pickles, hotdish or a cake
Often the call it comes in very late
With no time to spare a dish one must bake
It's always from scratch Now make No mistake!

Verse 3

A funeral, a shower Oh what will it be-
You come to church early and No one you see
The Kitchen's a mess, The League had the Key
Oh Lord I do ask you, is it all up to me?

LUTHERAN CHURCH BASEMENT WOMEN

Verse 1

The first words one hears when the telephone rings,
So sorry to hear that, now what can I bring.
The food that is brought in is fit for a king,
The humble reply is oh dats *ingenting.*

Verse 2

Sometimes it is pickles, hotdish or a cake,
Often the call, it comes in very late.
With no time to spare, a dish one must bake,
It's always from scratch, now make no mistake!

Verse 3

A funeral, a shower, oh what will it be,
You come to church early and no one you see.
The kitchen's a mess; the league had the key,
Oh Lord, I do ask you, is it all up to me?

Refrain:

OH-Us Lutheran church women we're none but the best,
We come in to serve from the east or the west.
The basement's our home; we will work night or day,
We clean and we cook the old fashioned way.

THE LADIES' AID

The old church bell had long been cracked; its call was but a groan,
It seemed to sound a funeral knell with every broken tone.
"We need a bell", the brethren said, "but taxes must be paid.
We have no money we can spare. Just ask the Ladies' Aid".

The shingles on the roof were old; the rain came down in rills,
The brethren slowly shook their heads and read the monthly bills.
The chairman of the board arose and said, "I am afraid
That we shall have to lay the case before the Ladies' Aid".

The preacher's salary was behind; the poor man blushed to meet
The grocer and the butcher when they passed him on the street.
But nobly spoke the brethren then, "Pastor, you shall be paid.
We'll call upon the treasurer of our good Ladies' Aid".

"Oh," said the man, "the way to heaven is long and hard and steep,
With slopes of ease on either side, the path is hard to keep,
We cannot climb the heights alone; our hearts are sore dismayed!
We ne'er shall get to heaven at all without the Ladies' Aid".

A KITCHEN PRAYER

Lord of all pots and pans and things,
since I've not time to be
A saint by doing lovely things
or watching late with Thee,
Or dreaming in the dawn light
or storming Heaven's gates,
Make me a saint by getting meals
and washing up the plates.

Warm all the kitchen with Thy love,
and light it with Thy peace,
Forgive me all my worrying
and make my grumbling cease,
Thou who didst love to give men food,
in room or by the sea
Accept this service that I do,
I do it unto Thee.

BEVERAGES

LUTHERAN BEVERAGES

COFFEE

Watkins Coffee for Fifty

3 eggs
1 pound Watkins Ground Coffee
2½ gallons boiling water

Beat eggs, add coffee and mix well. Add enough cold water to blend. Tie mixture in cheesecloth bag, add boiling water and boil 5 minutes. Lower heat, add 1 cup cold water and let settle 10 minutes over a low fire.

Egg Coffee

Bring to boil 6 to 7 cups water. Add 3 tbsp. coffee that has been mixed with part of an egg. Boil coffee until the foam disappears being careful so it doesn't cook over. Fill the remainder of the pot with boiling water. To settle the grounds, add a bit of cold water.

COLD DRINKS

Lemon Nectar Drink

Delicious, Refreshing Drink

2 tsp. Watkins Lemon Nectar Syrup
2 tsp. sugar
⅔ glass water

Blend syrup and sugar. Stir into water and add an ice cube.

Orangeade

2 cups granulated sugar
4 cups water
1 cup orange juice (strain)
⅓ cup lemon juice
2 oranges, peel, remove seeds and slice

Boil sugar and water to a syrup. Let cool, add juices, oranges and ice.

Watkins Cherry Nectar Drink

2 or more tsp. sugar
to taste
¾ glass cold water
1 to 2 tsp. Watkins Cherry
Nectar Syrup

Add sugar to nectar syrup and mix well. Add ice water, stir and serve.

Watkins Fruit Punch

¾ bottle Watkins Cherry
Nectar Syrup
¾ bottle Watkins Lemon
Nectar Syrup
½ bottle Watkins Orange
Nectar Syrup
5 pounds sugar
5 gallons water, ice cold

Blend Watkins Nectar Syrups and sugar and slowly stir in the water. A thin syrup may be made by boiling the sugar and water and when cold, stir in the Watkins Nectar Syrups. Serve with ice cubes.

Quick and Easy Punch

1 pkg. any flavored Kool-Aid
1 tray of ice cubes (12 cubes)
1 cup sugar

Dissolve Kool-Aid and sugar in tap water. Stir well. Add ice.
Serves 8.

For company, add a lemon slice. For silver wedding anniversaries, add 1 quart ginger ale to above mixture.

Campbell's
America's Favorite!
Tomato Juice
from concentrate
NET 46 FL. OZ. (1 QT. 14 OZ.) 1.36 LITERS

FANCY COCKTAILS

Tomato Juice Cocktail

To make a delicious tomato juice cocktail, add 1 tsp. Worcestershire Sauce, ⅛ tsp. celery salt and ⅛ tsp. pepper to each cup of tomato juice used. Mix, chill and serve.

Tomato Juice Cocktail

3 cups tomato juice
3 whole cloves
1 bay leaf
1 tbsp. minced onion
1 tsp. spicy meat sauce
2 tsp. sugar
3 tbsp. lemon juice
½ tsp. salt or less
Pepper

Simmer a short time, strain, chill and serve.

Everyday Lutheran Cocktails

Chill juice thoroughly. Serve in juice glasses when cold.

BREADS

"She needeth least, who kneadeth best, those rules which we shall tell. Who kneadeth ill, shall need them more than she who kneadeth well."

BREADS

White Bread

2 loaves

2 cups liquid
1 cake compressed yeast or
 1 pkg. fast granular yeast
2 tbsp. sugar
1 tbsp. salt
6 to 6½ cups sifted
 all-purpose flour
2 tbsp. shortening,
 melted and cooled

4 loaves

4 cups liquid
2 cakes compressed yeast or
 2 pkgs. fast granular yeast
4 tbsp. sugar
2 tbsp. salt
12 to 12½ cups sifted
 all-purpose flour
4 tbsp. shortening,
 melted and cooled

6 loaves

6 cups liquid
3 cakes compressed yeast or
 3 pkgs. fast granular yeast
6 tbsp. sugar
3 tbsp. salt
18 to 18½ cups sifted
 all-purpose flour
6 tbsp. shortening,
 melted and cooled

Method:

1. If using milk, measure, scald and partially cool. (Water or potato water does not need to be scalded.) Measure and melt shortening and let cool.
2. Crumble yeast into mixing bowl.
3. Add liquid at proper temperature.
4. Measure sugar and salt and stir in. Let stand until thoroughly dissolved, about 5 minutes.
5. Sift and measure flour. Add ½ of it. Beat with spoon until smooth and very elastic. (Batter will fall from the spoon in "sheets".)
6. Beat in melted and cooled shortening.
7. Add most of the remaining flour and work it in with your hands (possibly using the maximum amount) until the dough is possible to handle. Mix well.
8. Turn dough onto lightly floured board, cover, let stand 10 minutes to tighten up and then knead until smooth and elastic.
9. Round up and set to rise again until not quite double in bulk, about 45 minutes.
10. Punch down dough.

11. Round up and set to rise again until not quite double in bulk, about 45 minutes.
12. Punch down dough. Divide for loaves. Round up each part, cover and let rest for 15 minutes.
13. Mold into loaves.
14. Put in greased bread loaf pans. The dough should fill the pans ⅔ full. Cover with a damp cloth and let rise at proper temperature until sides of dough have reached the top of the pan and the center is well rounded out above the bowl (1½ to 2 hours). The dough should feel very light when touched gently with finger.
15. Bake 35 to 45 minutes. Bake in a hot oven (450 degrees) for the first 15 minutes and then reduce heat to a moderate oven (375 degrees) to finish baking. When baked, bread has a hollow sound when tapped and comes away from the sides of the pan.

Variations From Same Dough

(Ingredients for 2 loaves)

Nut bread – add 2 cups coarsely chopped nuts.
Date bread – add 2 cups cut-up dates.
Raisin bread – add 2 cups raisins (either seeded or seedless).
Cracked wheat bread – add 4 tbsp. honey and 2 cups cracked wheat.
Whole wheat bread – add 8 tbsp. molasses and 1½ cups whole wheat or graham flour.
Swedish Rye – add 4 tbsp. molasses, 4 tbsp. dark corn syrup, and 1½ cups rye flour. Bake at 375 to 400 degrees for 35 to 45 minutes.

A new Lutheran bride can't expect to make perfect Lutheran bread right away. Practice makes perfect and after some time a Lutheran woman doesn't even have to measure ingredients but goes by the feel of the bread.

Grandma's Water Rising Nut Twists

½ cup shortening
3 tbsp. sugar
½ tsp. salt
⅓ cup milk, scalded
1 tsp. vanilla
2 pkgs. dry yeast dissolved in ¼ cup warm water

Combine the first 5 ingredients and then add the yeast mixture.

1½ cups flour, blended in
3 eggs, beaten in 1 at a time

Cover and let rise for 15 minutes.
Blend 1½ cups flour into above mixture (3 cups flour in all)
The dough will be quite soft.

Grandma's way: Tie dough in soft cloth the size of a small dishtowel to allow dough to expand. Place in large bowl of warm water (75 to 80 degrees). Let stand to allow dough to rise to top of water (about 30 to 45 minutes). Remove from water. The dough will be soft and moist.

<u>My way</u>: Set bowl of dough in a warm place (80 to 90 degrees) for about half an hour covered.

Coating: 1 cup chopped nuts, any kind
¾ cup sugar
1 tsp. cinnamon

Stir this mixture on a large piece of waxed paper. Dip out rounded tablespoons of soft dough and roll in nut mixture. Either make a 3 or 4 inch long twist pressing ends down on a greased cookie sheet, or tie this long strip into a loose knot and place on cookie sheet (the latter keeps its shape better). Let stand for 10 minutes. Bake in a 375 degree oven over-browning on the bottom. Then put a shallow pan of water or a sheet of tinfoil on the lower grid. This makes about 25 mouth-watering delicacies that are convenient because they are served without butter.

History: Grandma used to make these for her church lady organizations. When her hands got too arthritic to be dexterous, she supervised me until I could turn out a product almost as good as hers. I have put down my modernizations here, but I still make them for my husband to take to church men's coffee hours when it is "his turn".
-Mrs. G. Gudmestad

Banana Bread

½ cup lard
1 cup sugar
2 eggs, well beaten
1 tsp. soda
3 tbsp. hot water
2 cups flour
¼ tsp. salt
3 bananas, mashed

Mix shortening, sugar and eggs. Dissolve soda in hot water and add one cup flour and salt. Add bananas and second cup of flour. Bake at 375 degrees for 45 minutes.

Do when bananas are 10 cents a pound. Stock up and bake like crazy. Freezes well. It's handy to have on hand.

Julekake (basic dough for any rolls)

1½ cups milk
½ cup sugar
2 cakes compressed yeast
5½ cups flour
1½ tsp. salt
2 eggs
¼ cup shortening

Scald milk and add sugar. Cool to lukewarm. Add yeast cakes and let stand 5 minutes. Add 3 cups flour, beat and then add salt and eggs and beat again. Blend shortening in and add remaining flour. Knead well and put in an oiled bowl to rise until double in bulk. Punch down and let rise again. Add currants, citron and candied fruit. Shape into a round loaf pan, let rise and bake. Frost with powdered sugar icing.

This makes more than 1 loaf, but we're not sure how many. This is made only at Christmas time in Lutheran circles. It is served only for festive events and not at funerals. It just wouldn't be appropriate.

Light and Airy Buns

1 cup lukewarm water
2 tsp. sugar
2 pkgs. dry yeast
3 small tsp. salt
2 tbsp. vinegar
3½ cups lukewarm water

½ cup sugar
½ cup shortening, melted
8 to 10 cups flour

Combine water, sugar and yeast. Let stand about 10 minutes. In a large bowl, put sugar, shortening, salt, vinegar, water and flour. Knead really well and let rise twice. Pinch off dough about the size of a crab apple. Place on a greased cookie sheet or cake pan. Let rise again. Bake 15 to 20 minutes at 400 degrees. Makes about 60 buns.

These buns were always served when the new pastor moved into the parsonage. Make them big for funerals and open face them. Great for Spam spread topping.

Limpa (Swedish Rye Bread)

2 cakes compressed yeast
½ cup water
1 tsp. sugar
1 cup sugar
½ cup shortening
3 tbsp. salt
½ cup molasses
1 cup water
1 tsp. soda
4 cups buttermilk
6 cups rye flour
8 cups white flour

Method: Dissolve yeast in ½ cup water and add 1 tsp. sugar. Combine sugar, shortening, salt, molasses and water and bring to a boil. Add soda to buttermilk and then add the hot liquid mixture. Add yeast when liquid is lukewarm. Add rye flour and beat thoroughly. Add enough white flour to make a stiff dough. Knead well and place in a greased bowl to rise until light. Knead down once and when light, shape into 6 round loaves. Place on greased tins and let rise until light. Bake at 375 degrees for about 45 minutes.

Variations: 2 cups of raisins may be added, if desired. Honey may be used in place of sugar for sweetening. The grated rind of 3 oranges may be added for flavor.

A favorite for Swedes, but Norwegians eat it, especially Norwegians that are Lutherans.

Mors Grov Brød (Brown Bread)

1 cake compressed yeast
4 cups lukewarm water
½ cup molasses
2 tbsp. salt
½ cup sugar
½ cup shortening, melted
9 cups white flour
3 cups whole wheat or graham flour

Method: Dissolve yeast in ½ cup lukewarm water. Let stand 15 minutes. Add 3½ cups lukewarm water, molasses, salt, sugar and shortening. Add enough flour to make a soft dough. Beat thoroughly for about 10 minutes and then add the rest of the flour to make a stiff dough. Knead and then place in a greased bowl. Cover and set in a warm place. When double in bulk, knead again. Let rise once more and then shape into loaves. Let rise until light. Bake about 45 minutes in a moderate oven. Brush tops with melted butter. Makes 4 medium size loaves. For delicious nut bread, try adding chopped walnuts to part of the dough. Bake as usual.

Every Lutheran Grandma knows this recipe. It's as basic as the 4 food groups.

Rye Bread

1 cake compressed yeast
2 cups warm water
¼ cup white sugar
⅛ cup brown sugar
1 tbsp. salt
1 egg, beaten
3 or 4 tbsp. molasses
2½ cups rye flour
4 tbsp. shortening, melted
4½ cups white flour

Crumble yeast in ¼ cup warm water and let soften for 5 minutes. Dissolve sugars and salt in remaining warm water. Add dissolved yeast, beaten egg and molasses. Add rye flour and beat well. Add melted shortening and white flour gradually to make a stiff dough. Turn on to a floured board and knead well. Place in greased bowl, cover and let rise in a warm place until double in bulk. Punch down and let rise again. Knead and form into loaves. Place in oiled pans, cover and let rise until light. Bake 10 minutes at 425 degrees and 40 minutes at 375 degrees.

Swedish Rye and rye are not one and the same. Promoters of Norwegian Lutheran lutefisk suppers sometimes feature Swedish Rye to get the ticket sales up.

Swedish Tea Ring

2 cakes compressed yeast
¼ cup lukewarm water
1 cup milk
¼ cup butter
½ cup sugar
1 tsp. salt
2 eggs, beaten
5 cups flour

Soften yeast in lukewarm water. Scald milk. Add butter, sugar and salt. Cool to lukewarm. Add flour to make a thick batter. Add yeast and eggs. Beat well. Add enough flour to make a soft dough. Turn out on a lightly floured board and knead until satiny. Place in a greased bowl, cover and let rise until double in bulk. When light, punch down and shape into tea rings, rolls or coffee cakes. Let rise until double in bulk (½ to ¾ hour). Bake at 375 degrees for 25 to 30 minutes for coffee cakes or 20 to 25 minutes for rolls. This recipe makes 2 (12-inch) tea rings or 3 dozen rolls.

Some Swedes really out-do themselves and gussy up this tea ring with maraschino cherries.

Three-Day Buns

1 cake compressed yeast
¼ cup lukewarm water
5 cups boiling water
2 tbsp. sugar
4 tbsp. butter, melted
1 tsp. salt
6 cups flour

Dissolve yeast in lukewarm water. Pour boiling water over sugar and butter. When cool, add salt, yeast and flour to make a stiff dough. Set dough in the icebox. Let rise twice and knead down. Let rise again. Form into buns and place on oiled pans. Let stand overnight. Bake in the morning for 20 minutes at 375 degrees. This recipe makes 3 dozen large buns.

If you have the time, these are good. Lutheran Women whose husbands are retired have time to make these. Some retired Lutheran husbands even watch them bake.

White Bread

1½ cakes yeast, compressed or granular
2¼ cups water
2 cups milk
¼ cup sugar
4 tsp. salt
11¾ cups bread flour
2 tbsp. shortening, melted

Crumble the yeast into ¼ cup lukewarm water and let soften for 5 minutes. Scald the milk. Add sugar, salt and cold water to the milk. Stir thoroughly until salt and sugar are dissolved. Pour into a large mixing bowl. Allow milk to cool until lukewarm. Pour softened yeast into the lukewarm milk mixture. Stir until well mixed. No chunks of yeast should remain separate after stirring. Add half of the sifted flour to the milk mixture. Stir the dough until flour and liquids are thoroughly mixed into a batter. (Note: Adding half of the flour at this time prevents streaks in the bread and helps to make a moist loaf which will keep fresh longer.) Melt the shortening. Allow cooling. Add to the batter and stir thoroughly. Add the remaining sifted flour and mix well. Stir flour into the batter until batter takes up the flour. After letting dough rest on floured board for 10 minutes, knead dough 12 minutes. Place dough in lightly greased bowl and allow to rise in a warm place approximately 2½ hours. Punch down and form into loaves. Allow rising until double in bulk. Bake this bread for 50 minutes at 400 degrees.

This recipe makes 4 loaves and is similar to another one in this book. If the other one doesn't work out, use this one.

Whole Wheat Bread

2 eggs
2½ cups rich sour milk or buttermilk
1 cup brown sugar
2 tsp. soda
2 cups white flour
2 cups graham or whole-wheat flour
2 tsp. baking powder
1 cup raisins, ground
½ tsp. salt

Beat eggs. Add milk and sugar. Add the sifted dry ingredients. Mix thoroughly. Add raisins. Place in an oiled pan and bake at 325 degrees for 1 hour. This makes 2 (5x9) loaves.

This is a hearty bread. Egg salad is good on this bread at home. Peanut butter and banana on whole wheat is a good treat but never served in a Lutheran Church. (The breads in this chapter are arranged alphabetically.)

PASS THE PICKLES PLEASE

Beet Pickles

Cook beets until tender. Slip skins and slice if beets are large. Place in clean hot jars, cover with boiling syrup and seal.

Syrup:
1 cup sugar
1 pint vinegar
A few whole cloves

These will add color to any table spread.

Bread and Butter Pickles

1 gallon cucumbers
2 green peppers
8 small white onions
½ cup salt

Select fresh, crisp cucumbers of dill pickling size. Wash but do not peel. Slice crosswise in paper-thin slices. Slice onions thin and shred peppers. Mix salt with the vegetables and bury pieces of cracked ice in the mixture. Cover with a weighted plate and let stand three hours. Drain thoroughly. In the meantime, make syrup as follows:

5 cups sugar
2 tbsp. mustard seed
1½ tsp. turmeric
1 tsp. celery seed
½ tsp. ground cloves
5 cups vinegar

Mix sugar, turmeric, and cloves. Add mustard seed, celery seed and vinegar. Mix well and pour over pickles. Put on low heat and heat to scalding but do not boil. Lift mixture occasionally with a paddle while heating. Seal in hot, sterilized jars.

These go well with funeral meals.

Chunk Pickles

Wash cucumbers and put in brine whole. (Brine is water with enough salt to float an egg.) Soak in brine 3 days. On the 4th day, drain off brine water and soak in clear water. On the 5th day, cut cucumbers in chunks and put them in a weakened vinegar solution with 1 tbsp. alum. Simmer for 2 hours. Add green food coloring. After 2 hours, drain off water and make brine of 2 cups vinegar, 2 quarts sugar and spices in a bag that consists of 1 oz. stick of cinnamon, 1 oz. whole cloves and 1 oz. whole allspice. After it comes to a boil, pour it over the pickles. This is enough brine for a dishpan of pickles. For at least 3 mornings after that, drain off brine and add 1 cup sugar and 1 cup vinegar. After the 3rd day, put in jars and seal.

These pickles go very well with minced ham spread on buns.

Crab Apple Pickles

Remove flower end of apple and replace with a clove. For 5 pounds of apples, use 3¾ pounds of sugar and a 5-cent box of stick cinnamon. (It costs a little more now.)

Place a layer of apples in a 1-gallon jar, then a layer of sugar and broken sticks of cinnamon. When jar is full, pour 1 quart vinegar over it. Put cover on jar and bake slowly 2 hours. When cool, place paraffin and paper over top and put away. Use stone jar.

Cucumber Pickles
Watkins Mixed Spices

Slice large cucumbers and cover with salt water overnight. Fill 2-quart jars with cucumbers. Add 2 teaspoons Watkins Mustard, 2 teaspoons sugar, 1 teaspoon Watkins Mixed Spices and 1 teaspoon celery seed. Fill jar with hot vinegar and seal in sterilized jars.

Cucumber Pickles

1 peck cucumbers
2 oz. black mustard seed
2 oz. celery seed
2 lbs. sugar
1 gallon vinegar
2 oz. white mustard seed
2 oz. juniper berries
½ quart small onions
½ dozen small green peppers
Watkins Mixed Spices

Put 1 peck of inch-long cucumbers in salt and water and cover tightly. Let stand 3 days. Put seeds in bags and boil with remaining ingredients for 15 minutes. Add a small piece of alum and pour over hot cucumbers that have been removed from the water. When cool, heat again several times until ready for use.

Cucumber Relish

1 qt. cucumbers
1 qt. onions
1 qt. cabbage
3 tsp. turmeric
Salt to taste
Watkins Mixed Spices
3 tsp. celery seed
3 tbsp. Watkins Dry Mustard
3 sweet red peppers
1 qt. vinegar
4 cups light brown sugar
½ cup flour

Peel and chop cucumbers and remove seeds (measure after chopping). Put all together and boil 15 minutes.

Syltelabber
(Pickled Pig's Feet)

Clean and scrape pig's feet thoroughly. Cut in halves lengthwise and cook in salted water until tender. Cook vinegar enough to cover with a ratio of ½ cup sugar to 3 cups vinegar and 1 cup water. Add pepper, whole all-spice and a few whole cloves for seasoning. Pour this solution boiling hot over the prepared pig's feet. When cold, place in refrigerator until ready to use. Let stand 2 days before using.

A real treat at Christmas.

String Bean Pickles

1 peck string beans
3 lbs. sugar
2 tbsp. dry mustard
2 tbsp. turmeric
3 pints vinegar
1 cup flour
2 tbsp. celery seed

Cut beans into uniform lengths. Cook ½ hour in salt water. Drain well. Mix dry ingredients with a little vinegar to form a smooth batter and stir this batter into the boiling vinegar to make a smooth paste. Add the beans, boil for 5 minutes and seal.

Sursild
(Pickled Herring)

4 large salt herring
1 cup vinegar
1 cup water
½ tsp. sugar
2 large onions
1 tbsp. whole pepper
6 bay leaves

Wash herring well. Skin and remove bones. Cut into small pieces. Mix vinegar, water and sugar. Add herring, sliced onions, pepper and bay leaves. Let stand overnight in a cool place.

A Norwegian favorite!

Watermelon Pickles

Peel and cut away pink center from watermelon rind. Cut into chunks about one inch long. Soak in salt water overnight. In the morning, drain the salt water. Boil until tender in clear water to which one tablespoon alum has been added. Drain and let come to a boil in clear water. Drain again. Boil in the following prepared juice for 15 minutes. Seal.

Juice:
5 cups vinegar
2 cups water
7 cups sugar
2 sticks cinnamon
1 tbsp. whole cloves
1 tbsp. whole allspice

Collect rinds after family reunion picnics.

JELL-O

Red and yellow, black and white, and green too.

ODE TO JELL-O

Every ethnic group would have a cheer,
The Germans toast, "Hail to our beer!"
Lutefisk and *lefse* can place the blame
On certain Scandinavians for their fame.

But a little-known food could find a place
In this never-ending battle for first place.
The cry could be heard from the young and old:
"Time to serve JELL-O – take it out of the mold".

Give me a "J" and an "E", double "L" and an "O",
Come on, you Norskies, you're moving too slow.
This is a salad, not a main dish,
Watch so it won't melt into the fish.

Bananas are an added treat
Carefully sliced into the JELL-O to eat,
Rise up and be counted as a true boy,
JELL-O is the dish that reminds you of joy.

It giggles and wiggles and bounces around;
It slips off your fork without making a sound.
You can always remember the last call each day:
"Did you all have your fill of JELL-O today?"

When relatives came, there was a new treat;
The JELL-O was topped with whipped cream – "Let's eat!"
"Not so fast", - I felt my hand sting – and it hurt!
"It's no longer salad – now it's dessert!"

So let's give a cheer for that American treat
That all Scandinavians soon learn to eat;
"Pass the JELL-O," I can still hear it said;
And remember the color – it has to be red!

RED JELL-O

Everyday Jell-O

1 small box Jell-O
1 cup hot water
1 cup cold water

Dissolve Jell-O in hot water. Add cold water and set. This recipe can be doubled.

A basic Lutheran Jell-O.

Jell-O for a Crowd

4 boxes Jell-O
4 cups hot water
4 cups cold water

Dissolve Jell-O in hot water. Be careful to get everything dissolved. Add cold water and refrigerate. When partially set, carefully slice in 1 good-sized banana or 2 small bananas.

This will feed about 30 people and is good for funerals or other doings. (This recipe was used for the 75th anniversary of the Trinity Lutheran Church.)

Company Jell-O

1 box red Jell-O (either strawberry or cherry)
1 cup hot water
1 cup cold water

Dissolve Jell-O in hot water. Add cold water and put in refrigerator to partially set. Slice banana. Follow directions for Jell-O for a Crowd. Before serving, top with whipped cream!

This is good for Sunday night supper when company drops in.

Rosy Vanilla Whip

1 pkg. raspberry flavored gelatin
2 cups water
1 pkg. vanilla pudding
2 cups milk

Prepare the raspberry-flavored gelatin with 2 cups water as directed on package. Prepare vanilla pudding with 2 cups milk as directed on package. Chill gelatin until slightly thickened. Chill pudding. Place the bowl of gelatin in a bowl of ice and water and whip with rotary beater until fluffy and the consistency of whipped cream. Add pudding gradually, beating constantly until blended. Turn into sherbet glasses or a large serving dish. Chill until firm. Garnish with cubes of clear gelatin or fresh fruit. Serves 10 to 12.

If you're gutsy, try other flavors of gelatin for variety.

Cranberry Salad

1 pkg. cherry Jell-O
1 cup hot water
1 cup cold water
½ lb. cranberries, ground
Nuts
Marshmallows

When dissolved and nearly cold, add ½ lb. freshly ground cranberries. When nearly set, add finely cut nuts and marshmallows.

A Lutheran Thanksgiving Jell-O.

YELLOW JELL-O

Cabbage and Pineapple Salad

1 pkg. lemon Jell-O
1½ cups hot water
2 cups chopped cabbage
1 cup grated pineapple
1 cup diced cucumbers

Dissolve lemon Jell-O in hot water, add to other ingredients and pour into mold. When set, turn out on lettuce to serve. Top with dressing.

Germans like this one!

Jell-O Dessert

½ cup sugar, divided
½ cup butter, melted
12 graham crackers, crushed
1 small can crushed pineapple
3 eggs, divided
1 pkg. lemon Jell-O

Make crust by adding 2 tablespoons sugar and ½ cup melted butter to 12 crushed graham crackers. Line pie tin. Add ⅓ cup sugar and the pineapple to the egg yolks which have been beaten thick. Cook in double boiler until thick and light in color. Pour boiling liquid mixture over one package of lemon Jell-O. Stir and mix well. Add 3 teaspoons sugar to stiffly beaten egg whites and fold into Jell-O mixture. Fill lined pie tin with Jell-O mixture and sprinkle with a crumb topping. Serve with whipped cream. To vary, use peaches, cherries, strawberries or raspberries. Use the same flavor Jell-O as the fruit. Serves 10.

Great for Circle!

Pineapple Set Salad

1 pkg. lemon Jell-O
1 cup boiling water
1 (No. 2) can crushed pineapple
1 cup pineapple juice
1 sm. jar pimento, cut fine
¼ cup grated American cheese
¾ cup diced celery
1 cup whipping cream
1 tbsp. salad dressing

Dissolve Jell-O in boiling water and add pineapple juice. When this starts to set, add pineapple, pimento, cheese and celery. Add whipped cream to which the salad dressing has been added. Whip all together. Chill. Serve on lettuce with mayonnaise dressing. Serves 12.

A wedding shower treat!

Salad Excellent

1 pkg. lemon Jell-O
1 lge. can crushed pineapple, drained
2 pkgs. Philadelphia Cream Cheese
1 sm. jar pimento
½ cup chopped celery
⅛ tsp salt
⅔ cup walnuts, chopped
½ pint whipping cream, beaten stiff

Boil pineapple juice and add to Jell-O. Let cool until slightly thick. Add the crushed pineapple. Mix cream cheese with pimento and add celery, salt and walnuts. Add to the Jell-O mixture. Fold in the whipping cream and place in the refrigerator until firm. Serves 10.

Black Cherry Jell-O Dessert

½ lb. vanilla wafers
1 lb. marshmallows
1 cup milk
1 lge. can pitted pie cherries
1 pkg. black cherry Jell-O
1 pkg. strawberry Jell-O
1 pt. whipping cream, whipped

Crush wafers fine. Cook marshmallows and milk until marshmallows melt. Let cool. Heat cherries to boiling point and drain. Add enough water to cherry juice to make 4 cups liquid. Dissolve the 2 packages of Jell-O in this liquid. When Jell-O starts to set, add cherries. Fold in ½ of the whipped cream (1 cup) into cooled marshmallow mixture. To mold, spread half of the crushed wafers in the bottom of the pan. Cover with marshmallow filling. Add Jell-O with cherries to form the second layer. For the third layer, whip the remaining cream, sweeten slightly and put on top of cherry layer. Sprinkle the top with remaining crushed wafers. Chill in the refrigerator until firm. If you want to slice your dessert, mold in a nut bread tin. Serves 16.

WHITE JELL-O

Yum Yum Salad

2 tbsp. gelatin
½ cup water
1 cup crushed pineapple
½ cup sugar
1 tbsp. lemon juice
1 cup grated cheese
2 tbsp. chopped green pepper
1 cup whipping cream

Soak gelatin in ½ cup water for ten minutes. Heat the crushed pineapple and mix well with the gelatin. Add the sugar and lemon juice. Chill until partially set and fold in the cheese, peppers and whipped cream. Pour into molds and chill until set. Serve garnished with lettuce and mayonnaise. Serves 8.

This goes good with lutefisk, lefse, and mashed potatoes if you prefer to keep all of your food white. Some Norwegian Lutherans like it this way.

Christmas Package Salad

1 pkg. lime Jell-O
1½ cups hot water
½ cup chopped celery
1 cup peas
1 cup finely shredded cabbage
½ cup grated carrots
Lettuce

Dissolve Jell-O in hot water, let set slightly and add vegetables. Pour into loaf pan, let set, cut in squares and serve on lettuce. Place strips of pimento across the serving of salad as if tied with a red ribbon. If a red salad base is used, decorate with strips of green pepper.

A clever Lutheran figured this one out.

Green Salad

1 pkg. lime Jell-O
1 cup cream, whipped
2 tbsp. chopped carrots
1 cup cottage cheese
1 cup Miracle Whip
Onions and olives, chopped as desired

Mix lime Jell-O according to directions, let set slightly and then whip. Add remaining ingredients and pour into molds and chill.

Can be served with or without mayonnaise, depending upon how fancy the people are that you are serving.

Jell-O Salad

1 pkg. lime Jell-O
1 pkg. lemon Jell-O
½ tsp. salt
1 tbsp. lemon juice
1 med. can pineapple
1 sm. stalk celery
1 med. can white cherries
1 sm. bottle stuffed olives, sliced
2 carrots, chopped fine
1 sm. cabbage, chopped fine

Dissolve Jell-O in 3 cups of hot water. Add all of the other ingredients and chill. Serves 12.

The white cherries make this a little "spendy".

Lime Salad

1 pkg. lime Jell-O
1½ cups boiling water
1 med. cucumber
3 med. carrots
½ green pepper
1 tsp. vinegar or lemon juice
1 cup cottage cheese
¾ cup whipping cream
½ cup salad dressing (Miracle Whip)

Dissolve Jell-O in boiling water. Cool until partially set. Grind vegetables and add to Jell-O mixture with the vinegar or lemon juice. Whip cottage cheese until smooth and combine with whipped cream. Add to Jell-O mixture and chill until set. Cut in squares and serve on lettuce with the salad dressing. Serves 8.

You be the judge.

Under-the-Sea Pear Salad

1 pkg. lime Jell-O
1½ cups boiling water
½ cup pear juice
¼ tsp. salt
1 tsp. vinegar or lemon juice
1 pkg. Philadelphia Cream Cheese
⅛ tsp. ginger
2 cups diced pears

Dissolve Jell-O in boiling water. Add pear juice, salt and vinegar. Pour half in mold and chill. Let the other half stand until jelly-like. Beat in cheese and ginger and fold in the pears. Add on top of other layer.

Some Lutherans call this Pharaoh's Army Jell-O.

Jell-O and Vegetables

1 box Jell-O
1 cup cold water
1 cup hot water
2 sm. or 1 lge. carrot
1 stalk celery
Salad dressing

Dissolve Jell-O in hot water. Add cold water and pour into aluminum mold. Refrigerate and when partially set, carefully add 2 small or 1 large grated carrot and 1 stalk chopped celery. Set until firm. Before serving, carefully remove from mold and serve with salad dressing.

This is good for showers.

JELL-O RECIPES AND TIPS THAT DIDN'T FIT IN THE OTHER CATEGORIES

Jell-O for Silver Weddings and Other Special Holiday Doings

3 boxes Jell-O
3 cups hot water
3 cups cold water

Dissolve Jell-O in hot water. Add cold water and pour into aluminum mold and refrigerate. When partially set, carefully add drained fruit cocktail, bananas, marshmallows or any other favorite ingredients for Jell-O. Before serving, carefully remove from mold and add whipped cream. Serve.

Jell-O Stretching

1 box Jell-O
1 cup hot water
1½ cup cold water

Dissolve Jell-O in hot water. Add cold water and set. This recipe can be used if you need a little bit more Jell-O.

Lutherans serve green Jell-O with fish.

Pineapple and rice

Refreshing and nice

Coleslaw

8 cups finely shredded cabbage
2 carrots, shredded
1 green pepper, chopped
½ cup finely chopped onion

Sprinkle vegetables with ½ cup cold water and place in refrigerator for at least ½ hour. Dissolve 1 envelope Knox Gelatin in ¼ cup cold water.

⅔ cup sugar
⅔ cup vinegar
1 tsp. celery salt
1 tsp. salt
¼ tsp. black pepper
⅔ cup oil

Mix sugar, vinegar and spices and bring to a boil. Stir in softened gelatin. Cool until slightly thickened. Beat well. Gradually beat in oil. Pour over chilled vegetables. This makes a large bowlful and keeps for days. Stir before each use.

Glorified Rice

1 box lemon gelatin
1 cup water
1 cup or less of crushed pineapple
2 cups dry rice, boiled
1 cup cream
4 or 5 tbsp. sugar
Salt to taste

Dissolve gelatin in boiling water. When cool and thickened, whip to consistency of heavy cream. Add the pineapple, rice, whipped cream, sugar and salt. Pour into any desired mold to set. When cool and set, unmold on serving plate. Garnish with whipped cream and red or green cherries. Makes about 10 servings.

Pineapple and Rice

2 cups cooked rice
1 cup drained crushed pineapple
24 marshmallows, cut-up
1 cup raw chopped apple
½ cup sugar
1 cup heavy cream

Cook rice in boiling salted water. Drain. Cool and mix with pineapple, marshmallows, apple and sugar. Place in refrigerator until serving time. Fold in cream that has been whipped. Garnish with candied cherries, sliced bananas or other fruit.

Mandarin Orange Salad

2 pkgs. (3 oz.) orange Jell-O
1 cup boiling water
2 cups vanilla ice cream
1½ cups hot water
1 can mandarin oranges and juice

Dissolve one package of orange Jell-O in one cup boiling water. Add two cups vanilla ice cream. Stir well. Pour into a 9-inch square pan and chill.

Dissolve one package of orange Jell-O in 1½ cups hot water. Add mandarin oranges and juice. Chill until syrupy. Pour over first layer. Chill. Cut into serving squares.

Mustard Ring Salad - 1940

2 tbsp. dry mustard
¾ cup sugar
Pinch of salt
¾ cup vinegar (fill with water to equal 1 cup
4 eggs, beaten

1 envelope gelatin
½ cup water to dissolve gelatin
1 cup whipping cream, whipped
1 to 1½ cups shredded cabbage

Mix dry ingredients and add vinegar/water mixture. Mix well and add beaten eggs. Dissolve gelatin in water in double boiler and stir until melted. Add egg mixture and cook until creamy, stirring constantly. Cool. Fold in whipped cream and cabbage. Pour into a greased mold or tube pan and refrigerate.

Simply delicious with ham!

HISTORY: The Sodality ladies ham dinner was memorable, not for its ham and good scalloped potatoes, but for its delicious Mustard Ring Salad.

Potato Salad for 100

Boil up 32 pounds of potatoes. Chill. Add 4 bunches of celery, 4 dozen hard-boiled eggs, 8 green peppers, pickles, salad dressing and salt and pepper to taste. Recipe can be doubled for big crowds.

A Sunday School Picnic MUST!

HOTDISHES

CHICKEN

Hotdish for Socials or Aid

1 medium chicken
1 cup diced celery
6 or 8 hard-cooked eggs, diced
1 tsp. salt
⅛ tsp. pepper
1 quart chicken broth
1 cup cream
4 tbsp. flour
1 tbsp. water

Cook chicken, remove bones and cut meat in small pieces. Butter baking dish and put in layers of chicken, celery and eggs until all are used. Add the cream to the chicken broth, bring to a boil and thicken with the flour, mixed with the water, until smooth. Pour sauce over the chicken mixture and top with cracker or bread crumbs. Bake until browned on top. Bake at 300 degrees for 1 hour. This serves 15 and is as timeless as you can get.

Mrs. P .W. (Peder Walter) Sorenson always skimped and used milk instead of real cream. Everyone could tell but never said anything. It wasn't the only thing she skimped on.

"Can Add Chicken" Rice Hotdish

2 cups cooked rice
½ cup chopped parsley
4 small onions
1 tsp. salt
2 cups grated cheese
2 eggs, beaten
3 cups milk

Mix rice, parsley, onions, cheese and salt. Mix eggs and milk and add to the rest. Bake in a buttered dish. Bake at 350 degrees for 1 hour. Serves 6-8.

To make this without chicken would be foolish. There would be nothing in the recipe that would stick to the ribs. This is especially important to remember when serving funerals where there are men eating.

Chicken Hotdish

1 chicken
1 pkg. ring macaroni
1 can peas
1 can mushroom soup
2 tbsp. butter
2 cups milk
2 tbsp. flour

Boil chicken until well done. Remove meat from bones and dice. Cook macaroni rings. Grease casserole and put macaroni, peas, diced chicken and mushroom soup in layers. Make a white sauce of the butter, milk and flour and pour over. Top with bread crumbs or shredded wheat. Bake for 40 minutes.

The shredded wheat gives this recipe some much-needed bulk. If you bake it too long, the peas become mushy.

Chicken, Veal or Turkey Royale
Fit for King Olaf

1 cup chopped mushrooms
4 tbsp. butter
1 tbsp. flour
½ cup bread crumbs
1¼ cups chopped, cooked chicken, turkey or veal
¾ cup milk
2 tbsp. chopped parsley
3 eggs
½ tsp. salt
Pepper

Dredge mushrooms with flour and brown in 2 tbsp. butter. Scald milk and add remaining butter and crumbs. Cool, add remaining ingredients and pour into buttered shallow pan. Set in a pan of hot water and bake at 350 degrees for 45 minutes or until firm. Cut in squares. Serve with cheese sauce.

Cheese Sauce

2 tbsp. butter
2 tbsp. flour
1 cup milk
½ cup grated cheese

Melt butter, add flour and blend. Add milk and cook over low heat, stirring constantly. Remove from flame and stir in cheese.

This isn't an everyday hotdish and is too time consuming to make for an ordinary church function. If the church higher-ups are visiting, this would be appropriate.

Chicken Hotdish

2 cups cooked chicken
½ can peas
3 cups cracker crumbs
1 cup cream
Chicken broth
Salt and pepper to taste
Grated onion, if desired

Alternate layers of chicken, peas and crumbs until dish is filled. Pour cream and broth over to cover the layers. Top with crumbs. Bake in a moderate oven about 40 minutes.

This is a basic chicken hotdish. Any kind of crumbs on the top will do.

Chicken Loaf

½ cup chopped green pepper
¼ cup butter, melted
1 cup cooked spaghetti
1 cup cooked, diced chicken
1 cup bread crumbs
1½ cups warm milk
¼ cup grated cheese
2 tbsp. chopped pimento
1 tsp. salt
3 eggs, beaten slightly
1 can mushroom soup
½ cup milk

Sauté green pepper in butter. Mix all ingredients except mushroom soup and ½ cup milk. Bake in loaf pan for 60 minutes. Slice and top with hot cream of mushroom soup diluted with milk.

This is pretty fancy and would be good for a shower – wedding or baby.

Escalloped Chicken

4 cups cubed chicken
4 cups broth
4 tbsp. flour
1¼ tsp. sage
¼ cup cream or chicken stock
¾ tsp. salt

4 tbsp. chicken fat
6 cups bread crumbs
¾ cup butter, melted
½ tsp. pepper
2 tbsp. chopped onion

Cook chicken in salted water, cool and cut into 1-inch cubes. Make a dressing of bread cut into 1-inch squares, melted butter or chicken fat, sage, stock or cream, salt, pepper and onion. Make gravy of broth, flour and chicken fat. Put 1½ inch layer of chicken in oiled pan. Cover with dry dressing. Pour gravy over top and bake at 375 degrees for 35 minutes.

This is a "meat and potato" chicken recipe and is good for potlucks.

Grandma Carlson's Chicken Hotdish

1 large chicken
1 cup diced carrots
1 cup diced potatoes
Salt and pepper to taste
1 can peas
1 small onion
1 cup diced celery

Cook chicken until done. Bone and dice chicken. Use broth to make gravy. Put all in layers in a casserole with a sprinkle of flour between layers. Add broth last and a little cream and bake.

This one could use this new store-bought Cream of Chicken soup. This is an old recipe so it could be changed.

GROUND BEEF

Corn Hotdish

1 lb. ground beef
1 small onion, chopped
2 tbsp. butter
1 can whole kernel corn
1 small green pepper, chopped
1 can tomato soup
½ tsp. salt
⅛ tsp. pepper
2 tbsp. flour
3 tbsp. water

Brown the meat and onion in the butter. Add the rest of the ingredients and simmer on top of the stove for 20 minutes. Use the flour mixed with the water for thickening.

If you have corn from your garden, all the better.

Dagne's Dinner in a Dish

4 tbsp. shortening
1 medium onion, sliced
2 green peppers, diced
1 lb. hamburger
1½ tsp. salt
¼ tsp. pepper
2 eggs
2 cups fresh cut corn
3 or 4 tomatoes
½ cup dry bread crumbs

Fry onions and peppers slightly. Blend in meat and seasoning. Remove from fire. Stir in eggs and mix well. Put a cup of corn in a buttered baking dish, cover with ½ of the meat and a layer of tomatoes. Repeat. Cover with bread crumbs. Bake for 35 minutes at 350 degrees.

If you don't have green peppers, skip it. Some men don't like them.

Glorified Hamburger

2 cups or 1 lb. hamburger
1 cup bread crumbs
½ tsp. baking powder
½ tsp. salt
Sprinkle of pepper
2 tbsp. catsup
Milk to moisten
Bacon

Mix crumbs, seasonings, baking powder and catsup with meat. Add enough milk to moisten sufficiently to mold into cakes. Put a strip of thin bacon around each and fasten with a toothpick. Put butter on top. Bake in a hot oven 45 minutes.

This is heavenly and fit for the angels. This isn't something that Lutheran Church Basement Women make for church doings, but Lutheran Church Basement Women do make it.

Hamburger Pie

1 lb. hamburger
1 large onion
1 can peas
12 potatoes
1 can whole kernel corn
1 can tomato soup
Salt and pepper
1 egg, beaten

Fry hamburger and onions stirring until brown. Put into a rectangular pan with corn, peas and soup. Season lightly with salt and pepper. Boil about one dozen potatoes and mash until fluffy. Add 1 beaten egg. Put a scoop of this over top of meat mixture for individual servings. Sprinkle with paprika. Bake in a hot oven about 20 minutes

Even though it might resemble apple crisp a la mode, it isn't. A clever way to serve meat and potatoes even though you can't technically call it a "hotdish". Mrs. Olaf Hanson thought this up when she was in the hospital recovering from pleurisy and other complications.

Hamburger-Rice Hotdish

Brown 1 lb. of hamburger and ¾ cup raw rice in 2 or 3 tbsp. fat. Put in a casserole with 1 cup of chopped onion, 1 cup of finely minced celery and 4 cups of tomato juice. Season with pepper and 1 tsp. each of curry powder and salt. Mix together thoroughly and bake, covered, in a moderate oven for 1½ hours at 350 degrees. Stir occasionally.

Some Lutheran women don't like or stock curry powder, so if you don't, it doesn't make any difference.

Helga's Hotdish

6 potatoes, sliced
4 onions, sliced
Salt and pepper
1 lb. hamburger
1 can tomatoes
1 can cream-style corn

Arrange potatoes and onions in baking pan. Season. Fry meat and add tomatoes and corn. Pour over potatoes and onions. Bake until potatoes are tender.

Sometimes when Helga brought this to Aid Meetings, she didn't bake it long enough and the potatoes were hard. Once persnickety Miss Esther Mae Skogen tried to cut the potato at Ladies Aid and it flew off her plate and landed in the late Mrs. A. K. Olson's lap. Everyone saw it and thought it's about time. She was always acting so perfect and criticizing everyone's kids.

Hot Hamburger Dish Supreme

1½ lbs. hamburger
2 tbsp. fat
1 onion, diced
2 cups fresh peas
2 cups raw, diced carrots
2 cups raw, diced potatoes
1 cup diced celery
1 can tomato soup
½ tsp. salt
⅛ tsp. pepper

Brown the meat and diced onion in the fat. Add vegetables, tomato soup, salt and pepper. Bake in a buttered baking dish. Bake at 350 degrees for 45 minutes

It serves 10 and is called "Hot Hamburger Dish Supreme" instead of just the hamburger dish because it calls for ½ pound more hamburger than the normal recipe.

Leftover Meat Dish

Make a regular bread dressing using about 4 or 5 cups bread crumbs. Grind up any leftover meats such as beef, veal or pork. Place about ½ of the meat in the bottom of a buttered baking dish. Cover with the dressing and the remainder of the meat and bake until slightly browned on top. Bake at 350 degrees for 35 minutes.

A good way to use up old bread and leftover meat and still have a tasty dish. Waste not. Want not.

Meat and Vegetable Hotdish

½ lb. pork
1½ lb. round steak
½ cup grated cheese
2 eggs
½ cup onions
½ green pepper, diced
1 cup cream-style corn
1 cup tomato soup
1 cup mushroom soup
Chow mein noodles

Grind pork and steak together. Mix with other ingredients and heat thoroughly. Serve on 1½ lbs. chow mein noodles.

It doesn't sound good to mix cream-style corn, tomato soup and cream of mushroom soup, but you can trust a tried and true Lutheran Church Basement Women's recipe.

Noodle and Hamburger Hotdish
For Funerals

1 lb. hamburger
1 onion
1 tsp. salt
⅛ tsp. pepper
1 pkg. egg noodles
1 can vegetable soup
1 can tomato soup
1 cup water

Fry hamburger and onions until brown. Add seasoning. Cook and drain the noodles. Mix together the meat, noodles and soups. Add 1 cup of water. Bake in a buttered casserole. Any leftover cooked vegetables may be added to this dish. Bake at 350 degrees for 1 hour.

If you don't have egg noodles, use elbow macaroni or any other sensible macaroni you have on hand.

Noodle Hotdish
For Funerals

5 slices bacon
1¼ lbs. hamburger
1 small onion, diced
1 can tomato soup
1 can peas and juice
½ cup mushrooms
½ tsp. salt
1 pkg. egg noodles

Fry bacon and remove from pan. Fry hamburger and onions. Add tomato soup, peas, mushrooms and salt. Mix all together and add noodles that have been cooked. Pour into buttered casserole. Place bacon strips over top. Bake at 400 degrees for 20 minutes.

Remember don't drain the peas! You need the pea juice for this one.

Six-Layer Hotdish

2 cups sliced raw potatoes
2 cups diced celery
1 cup diced onion
½ cup diced green pepper (optional)
2 cups tomatoes
1 lb. hamburger
½ tsp. salt
⅛ tsp. pepper (or less)

Arrange in layers with seasoned uncooked hamburger made into balls on top of dish. Bake at 350 degrees for 1½ hours.

If you skip the green peppers, which are optional, you only have a 5-layer hotdish; but Lutheran Church Basement Women still call it a Six-Layer Hotdish.

Sunday School Casserole

1 (6-oz) pkg. macaroni or spaghetti
¼ lb. dried beef
3 tbsp. butter
3 tbsp. flour
1½ cups milk
1 cup grated American cheese
1 green pepper, diced

Cook macaroni according to directions. Drain. Frizzle meat and cook green pepper in butter. Add flour and blend. Add milk and cook until thick stirring constantly. Add ¾ of the cheese. Combine sauce and macaroni. Top with remaining cheese. Bake 30 to 40 minutes at 350 degrees.

Only a Lutheran Church Basement Woman would know how to frizzle dried beef and frizzle it right. Sunday School kids like lots of cheese and no green peppers if you're making it for them.

Texas Hash

2 cups sliced onion
¾ cup chopped green pepper
3 tbsp. fat
1 lb. ground beef
1 tsp. salt
1 (No. 2) can tomatoes
½ cup uncooked rice
½ tsp. chili powder

Cook onion and green pepper in fat until onion is soft and yellow. Add meat and brown. Add remaining ingredients. Pour in greased casserole. Bake 1 hour at 350 degrees.

If you are a Lutheran from Texas, this might work out. If you're a Lutheran from the Midwest, the chili powder isn't going to win you any awards at most Midwest Lutheran functions.

Hotdish

1 lb. ground beef
2 lg. onions, sliced fine
2 green peppers, cut fine
3 tbsp. butter or Spry
2 cups canned tomatoes
½ cup uncooked rice
1 tsp. chili powder
1 tsp. salt
¼ tsp. pepper

Brown meat, onions and peppers in the butter and mix well. Add the tomatoes, rice, chili powder, salt and pepper. Bake in buttered casserole. Bake at 375 degrees for 45 minutes.

Tillie Thorstad moved from Decorah to Texas and started cooking different. She sent this recipe thinking we didn't have it in the Midwest. Evelyn Peterson thanked her for the recipe, but also told her that we already had the recipe and some had been making it for several years. She also added Midwest Lutheran Women didn't make it on a regular basis because people here work hard and can't afford to stay up all night with heartburn from chili powder.

PORK

Hotdish Deluxe

1 lb. lean pork
1 can chicken soup
1 cup water
2 small pkgs. noodles
1 small jar pimento
1 can cream-style corn
½ lb. cream cheese
1 cup bread crumbs

Bake at 325 degrees for 45 minutes.

Mr. And Mrs. Ole Ingebritson and their neighbors, Mr. And Mrs. Jens Olson went together and gave the pastor a half a hog for Christmas. The pastor's wife experimented around with all of the pork she had and came up with this recipe that she served when visiting pastors were guests in her home. Once when she brought it for Aid, everyone hinted for the recipe by telling her how delicious it was, but no one had the nerve to ask her except for Mrs. Andrew Olafson who dares to ask anything. The pastor's wife was gracious enough to give it to her.

TUNA

Potato Chips and Tuna Hotdish

½ lb. potato chips
1 (7-oz.) can tuna fish
1 small can peas
1 can mushroom soup
1 cup hot milk

Put alternate layers of potato chips, tuna and peas in a buttered baking dish. Add milk to the soup and pour over ingredients in casserole. Bake at 350 degrees for 1 hour.

This is good for a Dorcas Society lunch or any other light supper meal served in the church.

Snappy Tuna Ring

2 cups noodles, cooked
¼ lb. snappy cheese
1 can tuna fish
4 eggs
1½ cups milk
1 tsp. salt

Fill 1½ quart ring mold in layers with noodles, snappy cheese and tuna fish. Add beaten eggs, mixed with milk and salt. Place mold in pan of hot water and bake for 1 hour at 350 degrees. Unmold. Fill center of ring with buttered or creamed peas. Melt cheese to smooth sauce in double boiler. Pour cheese over top and serve at once.

The cheese is what makes this snappy. You'll need a lot of workers to serve this one so everyone can eat it hot. Everyone at Aid will ooh and aah over this one, that's for sure.

Tuna Fish Hotdish

1 can tuna fish
1 can mushroom soup
1 (10-cent) pkg. potato chips
2 hard-cooked eggs

Drain all oil from tuna fish, flake, and mix with the mushroom soup and crushed potato chips. Put in greased casserole. Place slices of hard-cooked eggs over top. Bake at 325 degrees for 45 minutes.

Potato chips have gone up in price since this was written, but what hasn't?

VEAL

Special Hotdish

1 lb. ground veal
1 onion, diced
1½ cups diced celery
3 tbsp. butter
1 small can mushrooms
½ cup rice
1 cup water
1 can cream of mushroom soup
1 can chicken rice soup
½ tsp. salt
⅛ tsp. pepper

Brown the onion, celery and meat in the butter. Add the mushrooms, rice, water and soups. Season with salt and pepper. Bake. The last ½ hour, sprinkle with ½ cup chopped salted almonds, if desired. Bake at 325 degrees for 1½ hours.

Mrs. Hans Olson said her sister-in-law's neighbor in Seattle had the church women serve this at her daughters wedding. (The sister-in-law of Mrs. Hans Olson sent the recipe to Mrs. Hans Olson.) She said the woman always lived beyond her means and always tried to impress everyone even though she was born and raised in a conservative Lutheran family. Lutheran Church Basement Women don't serve this in church, but some said they like to read how the other half of the world lives and cooks.

Chop Suey

18 stalks celery, diced
5 lbs. Bermuda onions, sliced
6 cups water or meat stock
3 lbs. veal, cut for chop suey
5 lbs. pork, cut for chop suey
2 tbsp. fat
3½ cups Chinese sauce
¾ cup molasses
2½ cups cornstarch
6 (No. 2) cans bean sprouts
1 lb. fresh tomatoes
2 green peppers
1 (¼ oz.) can pimentos
6 lbs. rice

Cook diced celery and sliced onions with water or meat stock until vegetables are soft but not completely cooked. Brown meat in 2 tbsp. fat. While meat is browning, drain liquid from celery and onions and mix the Chinese sauce, molasses and cornstarch. Cook on high until it boils and then add the meat and let sauce continue to cook until starchy taste is gone or about 30 minutes. Add the bean sprouts that have been drained, celery and onions and cook until thoroughly heated. Add the tomatoes, green peppers and pimentos that have been cut in thin strips. Serve on boiled rice or Chinese fried noodles. Serves 50 with a portion of ¾ cup each.

This isn't a favorite with Lutheran men but the world is getting smaller all the time and we can't live in our own little world.

Chow Mein

3 lbs. round steak
1 lb. veal
1 lb. pork
¼ cup lard or drippings
2 medium bunches celery
2 large onions
1 tsp. salt
1 tsp. pepper
1 (No. 2) can subgum
1 (8-oz.) can mushrooms
1 tbsp. molasses
1 (No. 2) can bean sprouts
3 tbsp. soy sauce
2 tbsp. flour
3 tbsp. water
3 cans noodles

Dice meat and brown well in drippings. Cook slowly with one cup water for 1 hour. Add celery and onions that are cut-up in small pieces, and the salt and pepper. Add remaining ingredients except the noodles. Thicken with 2 tbsp. flour mixed with 3 tbsp. water. Serve on hot crisp noodles. (For Chicken Chow Mein, use 3 lbs. diced chicken, 1 lb. veal and 1 lb pork.)

Some grocery stores don't carry subgum or bean sprouts, but you can get by without them. Chow Mein isn't served in the Lutheran Church, but it is gaining in popularity as an okay dish from the Orient. Someday in the future, it might be as popular as hotdishes.

Mexican Goulash

1 box spaghetti or noodles
1 lb. bacon
1 can corn
1 can tomatoes
1 can peas
1 can lima beans

Prepare spaghetti or noodles according to directions on box. Fry the bacon. Cut up and add it to the drippings. Then add corn, tomatoes, peas and lima beans. (Drain the liquid from the beans and peas.) Season to taste.

Lutheran Women use this recipe in a pinch.

Spanish Rice

¼ lb. bacon
1-3 cups chopped onions
3 cups boiled rice
2½ cups tomatoes
½ tsp. salt
½ tsp. celery salt

Cut bacon into small pieces. Brown in frying pan. Add onions and brown with bacon. Add rest of ingredients and pour in casserole and bake for about 45 minutes.

Most Lutherans prefer their rice "glorified". Some aren't comfortable with Spanish rice, but some are.

WHY LUTHERANS CALL THEIR DESSERTS "BARS"

Most Lutheran women have heard this story for years. As time went on, some fabrications and half-truths crept into this tale, but if you can overlook some minor exaggerations here and there, this story makes sense.

Once upon a time, Martin Luther's mother said to him, "Why don't you take Kitty and the kids up to Norway to visit my third cousin, Ingebrit Martinson, and her son Lars? She wrote me last Christmas and said she didn't know how much time she had left and she'd like you and your family to see their new Lutheran Church".

So, Martin and Kitty packed up Martin Jr., baby sister Olga, and some sandwiches and set off for Norway. Third cousin Ingebrit was so excited they were coming that she told all of her neighbors and they decided to honor Martin and his family with a potluck supper in the basement of their new Lutheran church – First Lutheran of Stavanger.

Meanwhile, Martin Luther's mother was glad to see Martin and his family go to Norway so she could have a little peace and quiet. Martin had created such a fuss in Germany, and she couldn't sleep. Even though she knew in her heart that Martin was "in the right", she was sure others were talking about him, and this caused her blood pressure to rise. (Martin's mother had a small amount of Norwegian blood in her veins that caused her to feel uneasy when anyone in her family was thrust in the limelight.)

When Martin and his family arrived at Ingebrit's home, everyone was happy and excited except Ingebrit's son, Lars. Famous people made him feel nervous and uneasy, and he didn't know how he should act. So he just acted the same, got up, and went outside to do the chores.

Ingebrit put on the egg coffee, brought out dried beef sandwiches, cheese, herring, buns, pickles, and desserts for a little snack. After Ingebrit apologized for not having ingenting on hand to serve, they all started to visit. Kitty was nervous because the kids were tired, crabby, and restless after the long journey. She was hoping they wouldn't act up too bad. Martin Luther's mother had warned Kitty to watch Martin, too.

He was always whistling "A Mighty Fortress", and in Norway, whistling was the same as calling the devil.

When Lars finished the chores, they all got ready and went to First Lutheran of Stavanger. Kitty was busy spit cleaning her children's faces with her hanky all the way to church. When they arrived, the church was full of men visiting, women cooking and children running and swinging around the church basement poles. The women in the kitchen, standing on their tiptoes, took turns looking through the little windows in the kitchen doors to try getting a glimpse of Martin and his family. Anna Axelson said she thought he wasn't as tall as she had imagined, but that didn't make him less of a Lutheran she supposed. "Oh my", said Tina Severson, "There he stands". Lena Larson said she didn't think Germans were usually as dark skinned as Martin and his family, but she added she'd never remembered seeing a real live German either.

Gurine Olson, President of the Ladies Aid, told the women to go to their assigned stations while she told the pastor "vær sa god". The pastor nodded to her and asked everyone to stand for the blessing and table grace. Everything went fine until they started to sing the last line of the table grace. Gurine Olson had invited all the neighboring Lutheran churches to the potluck, but because she was so busy getting everything ready, she forgot to ask the pastor to announce what ending to the table grace they would be singing. (Lutheran churches sing different endings.)

When some started to sing "May Feast in Paradise with Thee" while simultaneously others were singing "May Strengthen for Thy Service Be", Gurine turned beet red and got all embarrassed. She couldn't dwell on the embarrassment though, because she was in charge of getting everyone through the serving line. She knew Martin didn't know much Norwegian, nobody would explain it to him, and she would just have to think about it later when she went to sleep that night.

Everything went as smooth as could be expected until the desserts were passed around the table for a second time. By this time, the kids had gone outside to play, and only the grown-ups were left visiting and drinking coffee. After passing a plate of cake and desserts to the people sitting at Martin's table, Lena Larson scurried back to the kitchen and told everyone that Martin had said to her, "Those Prayer Bars are really good and hit the spot". Lena got all flustered, said "takk", and told the women in the kitchen she didn't know how to tell Martin Luther that a bar was not a dessert but a place where outlaws and ruffians would sit and drink hard liquor. Anna Axelson tried to calm down all the servers by telling them that maybe the word bar was the German word for dessert. Tina Severson said maybe Martin was just clearing stuff from his throat and Lena had just imagined Martin said the word bars.

While the women were discussing the issues, Kitty Luther walked into the kitchen and asked where the bathroom was located. She had Martin Luther, Jr. standing by her side – his clothes were all dirty and his nose was all bloody. Just then Lena Larson's son came running into the kitchen and said the kids were playing tombstone tag. Martin, Jr. had tried to jump over Hans Hauge's large tombstone but he didn't make it. He fell on his face and that's why, according to Lena Larson's son, he got hurt. Lena grabbed her son by the arm, sat him firmly on a chair, gave him that "wait until your father hears about this" look, and whispered in his ear to sit still if he know what was good for himself.

After a few minutes, Kitty Luther came back into the kitchen, thanked the women for letting her use the bathroom, and then to everyone's horror, asked Lena if she would be willing to part with her Prayer Bar recipe. Lena was flattered to be asked for the recipe, but couldn't muster up the courage to tell Kitty that Norwegians and Swedish Lutheran women didn't call their desserts – bars. She was so shaken that she didn't have any choice but to write down the recipe – "From the Kitchen of Lena Larson, Prayer Bars".

The rest is history. Since nobody dared to offend Martin Luther or his wife, Lutheran women had no other choice but to call their desserts "bars."

Apple Bars

Crust:

2½ cups flour
1 tsp. salt
2 tbsp. sugar
½ cup butter
½ cup shortening
2 egg yolks
Milk

Mix like pie crust. Put egg yolks into measuring cup and add enough milk to make ⅔ cup and add to first mixture. Roll out half to fit a jellyroll pan (about 10x15).

Filling:

⅔ cup crushed Corn Flakes
6 to 10 apples
1½ cups sugar
1 tsp. cinnamon

Sprinkle the Corn Flakes over the bottom crust. Slice apples and distribute over crust. Mix sugar and cinnamon and sprinkle over apples. Add the top crust and seal edges by pinching together.

Topping:

Beat 2 egg whites stiff and spread on crust. Bake 40 minutes in a 350 degree oven. Make a glaze of 1 cup powdered sugar and a little milk, flavored with vanilla. Drizzle over top while hot or melt light Kraft Caramels with ½ cup evaporated milk and use this instead of glaze. This may be used as a dessert or bar.

Aanna Olson said teenagers would clean up a pan of these bars quicker than lightening.

Chocolate Chip Bars

1 cup crunchy peanut butter
½ cup butter
1 cup chocolate chips

Melt together and pour over 1 bag miniature marshmallows. Put in a loaf pan and refrigerate. These will keep for a week, but then won't last a week. (Cool the chocolate mixture so it does not melt the marshmallows.)

Bran Date Bars

4 eggs, yolks and whites, beaten separately
1½ cups sugar
1 cup sifted flour
½ tsp. salt
2 tsp. Watkins Baking Powder
1 cup bran
¼ cup milk
1 tsp. Watkins Vanilla or Almond extract
1½ cups chopped dates
1 cup chopped walnut meats

Beat egg yolks and beat in sugar. Add sifted dry mixture alternately with milk. Add dates, nuts and lastly, beaten egg whites. Turn into shallow greased baking pan and bake in moderate oven. When cool, cut in strips and brush with powdered sugar.

A treat that helps you become "regular".

Brownies

1 cup butter
2 cups brown sugar
8 tbsp. cocoa
½ cup hot water
4 eggs
⅛ tsp. salt
1 tsp. vanilla
1 tsp. baking powder
1½ cups flour
1 cup nuts (or less)

Cream shortening, add sugar and cream well. Make a paste of cocoa and hot water. Add eggs, salt, vanilla and cocoa paste. Beat well. Sift baking powder with flour and add chopped nuts. Add to creamed mixture. Spread on buttered cookie sheet (14x17). Bake at 350 degrees for 30 minutes. Before brownies are completely cool, cut into desired size.

Everyone's favorite.

Coconut Bars

½ cup brown sugar
1 cup flour
½ cup butter

Blend together and pack in pan. Bake 10 minutes at 350 degrees. Mix the following and put on above after it is baked:

1 cup brown sugar
½ cup walnuts
1½ cups coconut
1 tsp. vanilla
2 eggs, beaten
2 tbsp. flour
¼ tsp. baking powder

Bake 20 minutes.

Little kids don't like these because of the coconut and walnuts.

Date Squares

1 lb. dates
½ cup water
½ cup sugar
1 tsp. lemon juice
1½ cups flour
¼ tsp. salt
½ tsp soda
¾ cup butter
1 cup brown sugar
1½ cups rolled oats

Dice dates; add water, ½ cup sugar and cook until mixture is clear. Add lemon juice and cool. Sift flour once, add salt and soda and sift together. Cream butter and add sugar gradually. Add rolled oats and flour and mix well. Place ½ of mixture in bottom of greased pan. Spread with date filling and cover with the remainder of the dough. Bake 20 minutes at 350 degrees. Cut in squares while warm.

Little kids won't eat these either.

Dream Bars

1 cup flour
½ cup shortening (half butter)
⅓ cup brown sugar

Mix well with hands. Pat in a 9x13 pan. Bake 10 minutes. Spread the following over the above mixture:

2 eggs, well-beaten
1¼ cups brown sugar
2 tbsp. flour
¾ cup coconut

Bake 20 minutes at 350 degrees. Cut into bars.

Lena says, "Quick and easy".

English Toffee

½ cup butter
1 cup brown sugar
Nuts – walnuts or pecans
Chocolate, bitter or sweet

Put butter and sugar in heavy saucepan and cook 12 minutes, stirring constantly. Pour over a layer of nuts in a buttered pie pan. Rub the surface with either bitter or sweet chocolate and shave a few nuts on top. When cold, break into small pieces.

Favorite of Episcopalians.

Lemon Bars

Mix 2 cups flour and ½ cup powdered sugar. Cut in 1 cup butter or margarine. Pat into a 9x13 pan. Bake 20 minutes at 350 degrees. Mix the following and spread over the first part:

2 cups sugar
4 eggs, slightly beaten
1 tbsp. flour
1 tsp. baking powder
4 tbsp. lemon juice

Bake for 25 minutes longer. Cut into bars when cool.

Gum Drop Squares

1 cup Crisco
1 cup brown sugar
½ cup white sugar
2 eggs plus 1 yolk
2 tsp. baking powder
¼ tsp. soda
1 tsp. salt
¼ tsp. cloves

1 tsp. vanilla
½ cup milk
2 cups flour
½ tsp. cinnamon
1 cup chopped gumdrops
1 cup chopped walnuts

Cream Crisco and sugar. Add beaten eggs and vanilla. Add milk alternately with sifted dry ingredients. Add gumdrops and nuts. Spread on a 12x16 cookie sheet to bake. Bake for 30 minutes at 375 degrees. Dust with powdered sugar before serving.

A special treat to give to the confirmation age kids after they've got their memorization down to snuff.

Honey Date Bars

1 cup honey
½ cup shortening
3 eggs
1 tsp. vanilla
1¾ cups flour
1 tsp. baking powder
1 tsp. cinnamon
½ tsp. nutmeg
1 tsp. salt
1 cup chopped dates
1 cup chopped nuts

Cream honey and shortening. Add well-beaten eggs and vanilla. Add sifted dry ingredients and beat until smooth. Add dates and nuts. Spread on an 11x17 cookie sheet to bake. Bake for 12 minutes at 375 degrees. Cut in strips and roll in powdered sugar.

Some call these "Holy Land Bars".

Marbled Brownies

1 cup butter
2 cups sugar
4 eggs
2 cups flour
½ tsp. salt
1½ tsp. vanilla
2 cups chopped walnuts
2 squares chocolate, melted

Cream butter and sugar. Add eggs one at a time, beating after each addition. Add flour, salt, vanilla and nuts. Divide batter in half and add melted chocolate to one half. Place batter by alternate spoonfuls in greased pan (8x8x2) and bake. Bake for 1¼ hours at 350 degrees.

When your brown sugar is either gone or hard as a rock – make these.

Marshmallow Bars

½ cup shortening (butter or margarine)
1 cup chunky peanut butter
2 - 6 oz. pkgs. Butterscotch or Toll House Morsels

Melt in double boiler and cool until nearly lukewarm.

Fold in:

¾ cup flaked coconut
1 pkg. colored miniature marshmallows
½ cup nut meats may be added if using the cream-style peanut butter

Cool and cut in squares. May be stored in the refrigerator for an indefinite time. Use 9x13 pan.

Nut *Goodies*

1 cup sugar
½ cup butter
2 eggs
1½ cups flour (scant)
1 tsp. baking powder
½ tsp. vanilla
½ cup chopped nuts

Cream sugar and butter. Add beaten eggs, flour, baking powder and vanilla. Spread in buttered pan and cover with nuts. Spread the following mixture over the first part:

1 cup brown sugar
2 egg whites
½ tsp. vanilla

Fold brown sugar and vanilla into beaten egg whites. Bake for 30 minutes at 350 degrees. Cut in squares and remove from pan to cool.

Good as "store bought" candy bars.

Oatmeal Bars

1 cup oatmeal
1¼ cups boiling water

Stir and let stand for 20 minutes.

½ cup butter
1 cup brown sugar
1 cup white sugar
2 eggs
1 tsp. vanilla
1½ cups flour
1 tsp. soda
¼ tsp. salt

Cream butter and sugars. Add eggs and vanilla. Add cooled oatmeal mixture and dry ingredients. Bake on a cookie sheet or 10x14 cake pan for 25 minutes at 350 degrees.

Topping:

½ cup butter
6 tbsp. Carnation Milk or cream
1½ cups brown sugar

Boil for 2 minutes and then add ½ cup nuts and 1 cup coconut. Beat and spread on while warm.

Orange Slice Bars

Mix ½ cup butter, ½ cup brown sugar, a dash of salt and 1 cup flour. Press into a 9x13 ungreased pan. Bake 10 minutes at 375 degrees. Then spread the following mixture over the bottom layer:

2 eggs, well beaten
1 cup brown sugar
1 tsp. vanilla
2 tbsp. flour
1 tsp. baking powder
Dash of salt
1 cup shredded coconut
1 cup cut-up orange slices
1 cup nuts (optional)

Bake for 25 minutes at 350 degrees.

Make in winter when citrus fruit is in season.

Peanut Butter Bars

1 cup white syrup
2 cups sugar
1 cup peanut butter
6 cups Corn Flakes

Mix syrup and sugar together until melted over burner. Shut off stove and add 1 cup peanut butter and mix well. Add 6 cups Corn Flakes (as they come from the box – do not crush). Put in greased 9x13 pan. Cut when cool.

Easy as pie.

Prayer Bars

First layer:
5 tbsp. cocoa
¼ cup butter

Melt over hot water and add:
½ cup powdered sugar
1 egg, slightly beaten
1 to 2 tsp. vanilla

Mix 2 cups crushed graham crackers, ½ cup nuts and 1 cup coconut. Add to first mixture and mix well. Press into a 9x13 inch pan. Chill.

Second layer:
¼ cup butter
3 tbsp. cream
1 tsp. vanilla
2 tsp. dry pudding
2 cups powdered sugar

Melt and add 2 tsp. dry pudding mix. Remove from heat and add 2 cups powdered sugar. Blend well and spread on the first layer.

Third layer:
1¾ oz. chocolate bar

Melt chocolate bar and spread over top. Bring to room temperature before cutting. Store in refrigerator.

A favorite of Martin Luther.

Spice Bars

1 cup brown sugar
¾ cup shortening
2 eggs
½ cup molasses
2 cups flour
1 tsp. soda
1 tsp. cloves
1 tsp. cinnamon
½ tsp. ginger
¼ tsp. salt
1 cup hot coffee

Bake at 325 degrees for 15 minutes. Frost.

Sugar and spice and everything nice.

Sugarless Brownies

1 cup Karo Syrup
½ cup shortening
1 tsp. vanilla
2 squares chocolate
¾ cup flour
¼ tsp. salt
½ tsp. baking powder
2 eggs
½ cup chopped nutmeats

Beat together the syrup, shortening, vanilla and melted chocolate. Sift the flour, salt and baking powder. Add ¼ cup of the flour mixture, the well-beaten eggs and the rest of the flour and nuts. Spread on a cookie sheet, and when baked, cover with the following frosting:

1 cup powdered sugar
1 tbsp. butter
1 egg white
1 tbsp. cocoa
1 tsp. vanilla

Beat together until creamy and spread. Bake for 35 minutes at 350 degrees. Cut in squares.

When you run out of sugar, these are the tricks.

Tutti-Frutti Squares

¾ cup flour
1 cup chopped nuts
¾ cup sugar
1 tsp. baking powder
2 eggs
½ tsp. salt
1 cup sliced dates
3 tbsp. melted fat
¼ cup each: candied citron, orange peel and cherries

Spread ¾" thick in well-greased shallow pan lined with wax paper. Bake in slow oven until firm to touch, about ¾ to 1 hour.

A fancy name for a fancy bar.

Walnut Sticks

¼ cup butter or Crisco
1 cup light brown sugar
1 tsp. vanilla
⅛ tsp. salt
1 egg
½ cup black walnuts
1 cup flour
1 tsp. baking powder

Bake 30 minutes. Makes 16 squares in an 8x8 pan.

Grown-up bars.

Walnut Strips

Crust:
½ cup shortening
1 cup flour

Mix and pat into bottom of 8x14 pan. Bake 12 to 15 minutes.

Filling:
2 eggs
1½ cups brown sugar
2 tbsp. flour
¼ tsp. baking powder
½ tsp. salt
½ cup chopped walnuts
½ cup coconut (optional)
1 tsp. vanilla

Mix in order given and spread on crust. Return to oven and bake 15 to 20 minutes.

Frosting:

2 tbsp. butter
1½ cups powdered sugar
2 tbsp. warm orange juice
1 tsp. lemon juice

Beat together until creamy and spread on cake. Bake for 30 minutes at 350 degrees. Cut in squares.

CAKES

BIBLE CAKES

Bible Cake

4½ cups flour	I Kings 4:22
1 cup butter	Judges 5:22 (last clauses)
2 cups sugar	Jeremiah 6:20
2 cups raisins	I Samuel 30:12
2 cups figs	Nahum 3:12
2 cups honey	I Samuel 14:25
Pinch of salt	Leviticus 2:13
6 eggs	Jeremiah 17:11
½ cup milk	Judges 4:19 (last clauses)
2 cakes leaven	Amos 4:15
Season to taste of spice	II Chronicles 9:19

Some Lutheran church cookbooks call this Scripture Cake and make you look up the passages. We've saved you some work!

These good old "stand-bys" are baked when you're under the gun, on the run, with too much work that needs to be done.

Apple Upside-Down Cake

2 eggs
1 cup sugar
1 cup flour
1 tsp. baking powder
¼ tsp. salt
½ cup cold water
1 tsp. vanilla
3 to 4 apples, peeled and sliced
1 cup sugar (for apples)
1 tsp. cinnamon

Beat eggs and beat the sugar into the eggs. Sift flour once before measuring and sift flour, baking powder and salt. Add to egg mixture alternately with the water. Add vanilla. Cover the bottom with sliced apples, mixed with 1 cup sugar and the cinnamon. Bake in a buttered 9-inch square pan. Serve hot with whipped cream.

Make in the fall of the year when apples are plenty.

Crumb Cake

2 cups brown sugar
½ cup butter
2 cups flour
2 eggs
1 cup sour milk or buttermilk
1 tsp. soda
1 tsp. vanilla
½ cup nuts

Mix sugar, butter and flour together, as for pie crust. From this, take out ¾ cup for crumbs for frosting. Then add eggs and milk to which soda has been added. Add vanilla and nuts and beat for 10 minutes. Sprinkle remaining crumbs on unbaked cake. Bake in loaf pan.

Spice Cake

½ cup shortening
1½ cups sugar
3 eggs, divided
2¼ cups flour
3 tsp. baking powder
½ tsp. salt
1 tsp. cinnamon
½ tsp. cloves
½ tsp. nutmeg
¼ tsp. allspice
1 cup milk
1 tsp. vanilla

Cream shortening and add sugar gradually. Beat egg yolks until lemon-colored and add to creamed mixture. Sift all dry ingredients and add alternately with the milk. Beat egg whites stiff and fold in last, together with the vanilla. Bake at 350 degrees for 40 minutes if it's a loaf and 25 minutes if it's a layer.

Velvet Lunch Cake

½ cup butter
1 cup brown sugar
1 egg
1 tsp. soda
1 cup sour milk
2 cups flour sifted with:
1 tsp. cinnamon
¼ tsp. cloves
¼ tsp. nutmeg

Cream shortening and sugar and add egg. Beat thoroughly. Add flour and spices alternately with the sour milk. Bake in 2 greased 8- inch pans in a moderate oven at 375 degrees.

Good for a man's lunch box.

Rhubarb Cake

1½ cups brown sugar
½ cup shortening
1 egg
1 cup sour milk or buttermilk
2 cups flour
1 tsp. vanilla
1 tsp. soda
¼ tsp. salt
1½ cups rhubarb (cut fine)

Cream sugar and shortening. Beat in egg. Add rest of ingredients. Pour in pan (7x11x2). On top, sprinkle ½ cup sugar mixed with ½ tsp. cinnamon. Bake at 350 degrees for 45 minutes. Serve with whipped cream or ice cream.

Cherry Cake

¾ cup shortening
1½ cups sugar
½ tsp. vanilla
¼ tsp. lemon extract
½ cup finely chopped cherries
3 cups cake flour
3 tsp. baking powder
¼ tsp. salt
1 cup milk
4 egg whites

Cream shortening and sugar. Add flavorings and well-drained cherries. Alternate adding sifted dry ingredients with milk. Fold in well-beaten egg whites. Pour in pan and bake.

Cherry Coconut Cake

1 cup flour
2 tbsp. sugar
½ cup butter

Mix with fork and bake in moderate oven for 10 minutes in an 11-inch square pan.

Spread with following topping.

1 cup sugar
2 eggs, beaten
¼ cup flour
½ tsp. baking powder
Pinch of salt
1 tsp. vanilla
1 (8-oz.) jar maraschino cherries
½ of juice from jar of cherries
1 cup coconut

Bake in moderate oven about 20 minutes or until done.

Devils Food Cake

2 cups sifted cake flour
1 tsp. soda
¼ tsp. salt
1½ cups brown sugar
½ cup butter
2 eggs
3 squares chocolate (melted)
1 cup sweet milk
1 tsp. vanilla

Add soda and salt to flour and sift twice. Cream butter and sugar until light. Add eggs, one at a time, beating well after each addition. Add melted chocolate. Alternately, add flour with milk and vanilla. Bake at 350 degrees for 45 minutes in a 9x9 square pan.

Mayonnaise Cake

1 tsp. soda
1 cup boiling water
1 cup chopped dates
1 cup chopped nuts
1 cup sugar
¾ cup mayonnaise (no other)
1 tsp. vanilla
2 cups flour
1 tsp. cinnamon
2 tbsp. ground chocolate

Mix soda and water and pour over dates and nuts. Let stand while mixing the other ingredients. Mix sugar, mayonnaise and vanilla, gradually adding flour, cinnamon and chocolate. Combine all and mix well. Bake in a moderate oven.

Marble Cake

White Part:
3 tbsp. shortening
½ cup sugar
½ tsp. lemon extract
½ cup milk
1 cup flour
2 tsp. baking powder
¼ tsp. salt
White of one egg

Dark Part:
3 tbsp. shortening
½ cup sugar
Yolk of one egg
½ cup milk
1 cup flour
2 tsp. baking powder
¼ tsp. salt
½ tsp. cloves
½ tsp. nutmeg
1 tsp. cinnamon
2 tbsp. cocoa

Use 2 bowls – Part 1: Cream shortening, add sugar slowly and add flavoring and milk. Beat well and add flour sifted with salt and baking powder. Fold in beaten egg white. Part 2: Cream shortening, add sugar slowly and then egg yolk and mix well. Add milk and flour with baking powder, salt, spices and cocoa that has been sifted together. Put both batters by spoonfuls alternately into greased pans, but do not mix. Bake in moderate oven about 45 minutes. Cover with white icing.

Marble Cocoa Cake

1 cup sugar
½ cup butter
½ tsp. baking powder
2 cups flour (sifted 5 times)
1 cup milk
½ tsp. vanilla
3 egg whites

Cream butter and sugar. Sift baking powder and flour and add milk alternately with flour. Add flavoring and beaten egg whites. Separate the batter and to ½ of it, add: 3 tsp. cocoa, ½ tsp. each of nutmeg, allspice and cinnamon, and ¼ tsp. of soda. Beat well and drop in buttered pan, first 1 spoonful of white batter and then a spoonful of dark until it's used up.

Orange Cake

1 cup sugar
½ cup shortening
Rind of ½ orange
2 eggs
2 cups flour
1 tsp. baking powder
1 tsp. soda
⅛ tsp. salt
1 cup raisins
1 cup sweet milk
Juice of 1 orange

Cream sugar, shortening and orange rind. Add well-beaten eggs. Sift flour, soda, baking powder and salt. Grind or cut up raisins and dredge with ¼ cup of the flour. Add dry and liquid ingredients to creamed mixture. Add raisins last. Bake at 350 degrees in a 9x9 square pan for 45 minutes.

Prune Cake

½ cup butter
1 cup sugar
2 eggs
1 tsp. cinnamon
1 tsp. vanilla
2 cups sifted cake flour
½ tsp. cloves
1 cup cut-up prunes (cook before) – no juice
1 cup buttermilk with
1 tsp. soda

Cream butter and sugar. Add remaining ingredients. Bake 30 minutes at 350 degrees. Frost with white icing (recipe elsewhere in chapter) and cut in 4" pieces.

Good for funerals.

Watkins Chocolate Dessert Cake

1 egg
1 cup sugar and 2 tbsp. shortening creamed together
1½ cups flour
¼ tsp. salt
½ cup Watkins Chocolate Dessert
2 tsp. Watkins Baking Powder
1 tsp. Watkins Vanilla

Break egg into cup and fill with milk and beat. Add sugar and shortening. Sift flour, salt, Watkins Chocolate Dessert and baking powder together and add to first mixture. Add 1 tsp. Watkins Vanilla. Bake in layers at 375 degrees for 25 minutes. Use your favorite frosting.

BASIC ICING RECIPES

White Icing

1 cup sugar
½ cup water
2 egg whites, beaten stiffly
1 tsp. vanilla

Cook the sugar and water in a small saucepan until it spins a thread. Pour the sugar and water mixture into the beaten egg whites and beat until glossy. Add vanilla and beat again. Spread on cake.

Chocolate Icing

⅓ square chocolate
2 tbsp. milk or cream
1 cup powdered sugar

Melt chocolate, add to sugar and moisten with liquid.

Chocolate Mocha Cake

½ cup butter
1 cup sugar
1 egg
1 tsp. vanilla
1 tsp. soda
2 tbsp. cocoa
1 cup sour milk
1½ cups flour
2 tsp. baking powder

Cream butter, add sugar, then egg and beat until light. Add soda and cocoa and sour milk. Work in flour with baking powder and beat 100 times. Bake in a slow oven.

Cream Cake

1¼ cups cake flour
2 tsp. baking powder
⅛ tsp. salt
1 cup sugar
4 eggs, well beaten
⅓ cup sweet cream
1 tsp. lemon flavoring

Sift flour, measure, and sift with baking powder and salt. Combine sugar, eggs and cream. Stir until well blended. Add flavoring. Add dry ingredients. Beat 5 minutes. Pour into a well-oiled shallow pan. Bake in a 375 degree oven for 30 minutes.

Daffodil Cake

1 cup cake flour
½ cup sugar
1⅓ cups egg whites
¼ tsp. salt
1¼ tsp. cream of tartar
1 cup sugar
1 tsp. vanilla
½ tsp. almond extract
4 egg yolks, well beaten
2 tbsp. cake flour
1 tsp. lemon extract
1 tsp. vanilla

Sift 1 cup flour with ½ cup sugar three times. Beat egg whites until frothy. Add salt and cream of tartar. Beat until stiff, but still glossy. Add the 1 cup sugar gradually. Add vanilla and lemon extract. Fold in the flour mixture gradually. Divide the batter in 2 parts. In one half, fold egg yolks, 2 tbsp. flour and lemon extract. Fold vanilla in the other half.

Spoon batter alternately into a 10-inch ungreased tube pan. Bake at 325 degrees for 1 hour.

A good cake to serve at Spring Ladies Aid Banquets. Some plastic daffodil and tulip centerpieces would make a good compliment to this cake.

Gold Cake

1½ cups sugar
½ cup water
6 eggs, beaten separately
¼ tsp. salt
1¼ cups flour
1 cup cake flour
¾ tsp. cream of tartar
1 tsp. lemon or orange extract

Boil sugar and water until it threads when dropped from the tip of the spoon. Pour the hot syrup in a fine stream over the beaten egg white to which salt has been added, beating mixture until cool. Add the well-beaten egg yolks. Sift the flour once, measure, and add cream of tartar and sift again 3 times. Fold carefully into egg mixture. Add extract. Pour into ungreased tube pan and bake 50-60 minutes in a moderately slow oven (325-350 degrees). When done, invert to cool.

Lady Baltimore Cake

½ cup butter (cream butter and sugar
1⅓ cups sugar
1 cup milk
½ cup sifted cake flour
Vanilla flavor
4 well-beaten egg whites

Bake.

Filling for Cake:
6 tbsp. sugar
2 tbsp. corn starch
1 lemon (grated)
½ cup cold water
4 egg yolks
Salt

Cook in double boiler and when cool, spread between layers of cake. A white frosting on top and over all makes a fine party finish.

Old-Fashioned Jelly Roll

¾ cup sifted cake flour
¾ tsp. baking powder
¾ cup sugar
4 eggs
¼ tsp. salt
1 tsp. vanilla
1 cup jelly (any flavor)

Sift flour once and measure. Combine baking powder, salt and eggs in bowl. Place over small bowl of hot water and beat with rotary beater, adding sugar gradually until mixture becomes thick and light colored. Remove bowl from hot water. Fold in flour and vanilla. Turn into greased pan, 15x10 inches, lined with greased paper and bake at 400 degrees for 13 minutes. Quickly cut off crisp edges of cake. Turn from pan at once onto cloth covered with powdered sugar. Remove paper. Spread with jelly, almost to edge. Roll quickly. Wrap in cloth and cool on rack.

Rich White Cake

1¼ cups sugar
½ cup butter
½ cup milk
3 egg whites, beaten
2 cups flour
2 tsp. baking powder

Cream sugar and butter and add milk and egg whites. Sift flour and baking powder together 3 times. Flavor with lemon juice and vanilla. Bake.

Spring Beauty Cake

1 cup sifted cake flour
1 tsp. baking powder
¼ tsp. salt
3 eggs
1 cup sugar
2 tsp. lemon juice
6 tbsp. hot milk

Sift flour, baking powder and salt together 3 times. Beat eggs with rotary eggbeater until thick enough to stand up in soft peaks (5 to 7 minutes). Add sugar gradually, beating constantly. Add lemon juice. Fold in flour, a small amount at a time. Add hot milk and stir quickly until thoroughly blended. Turn at once into an ungreased tube pan and bake in moderate oven (350 degrees) for 35 minutes or until done. Invert pan for 1 hour or until cool. Remove from pan and pile strawberry fluff topping on top of cake.

Strawberry Fluff Frosting

Combine 1 egg white, unbeaten, ½ cup sugar, dash of salt and ⅓ cup sliced strawberries in top of double boiler and beat with rotary eggbeater until thoroughly mixed. Place pan over rapidly boiling water, beat constantly with rotary beater and cook 3 minutes, or until mix will stand in soft peaks. Remove from heat and fold in
⅓ cup sliced strawberries.

Snow Cake

¼ cup butter
1 cup white sugar
½ tsp. vanilla
2 egg whites
1⅔ cups flour
1 rounded tsp. baking powder
½ cup milk

Cream butter, sugar and vanilla. Beat egg whites to stiff froth. Sift flour and baking powder thoroughly. Add to first mixture with milk and lastly fold in egg whites. Cover with boiled icing.

ANGEL FOOD CAKES

Angel Food Cake

1½ cups sugar
1⅛ cups cake flour
⅛ tsp. salt
12 egg whites, very cold
1 tsp. cream of tartar
½ tsp. any flavoring

Sift and measure sugar and flour separately and sift each 4 more times. Add salt to egg whites and beat until foamy. Add cream of tartar and beat until egg whites hold their shape when bowl is inverted. Add sugar slowly, folding in. Add flavoring and fold in flour carefully. Baking time is 50 minutes. Put in slow oven (150 degrees) and increase heat gradually until last 15 minutes are 350 degrees.

Chocolate Angel Food Cake

⅛ tsp. salt
1½ cups egg whites
1 tsp. cream of tartar
1½ cups sugar, sifted
¾ cup sifted cake flour
¼ cup cocoa
1½ tsp. vanilla

Add salt to egg whites, beat until foamy, add cream of tartar and beat until whites will hang to beater. Then fold in sugar slowly – in the same manner as in making mush, by taking handfuls and letting it sift slowly through the fingers. Fold in flour and cocoa. Add flavoring. Bake for 30 minutes at 300 degrees and 30 minutes at 350 degrees until done.

Orange Angel Food Cake

8 eggs, divided
1½ cups sifted sugar
Grated rind of 1 orange
½ tsp. lemon juice
⅓ cup orange juice
1½ tsp. vanilla
½ tsp. cream of tartar
1½ cups sifted cake flour

Beat yolks until lemon-colored. Add ¾ of the sugar gradually, rind, juices and flavoring. Beat egg whites as for angel food. Add cream of tartar when frothy. Add the rest of the sugar gradually to the whites. Fold in egg yolk mixture and then fold in the flour, which has been sifted before measuring and sifted several times after measuring. Bake at 350 degrees for 1 hour.

Mock Angel Food Cake

1½ cups sugar
2 cups cake flour
1 cup boiling water
½ tsp. vanilla
5 egg whites
¼ tsp. salt
1 tsp. cream of tartar
2 tsp. baking powder

First mix sugar and flour after sifting once. Into this, pour the boiling water while stirring well. Let it cool before starting the rest. Then, beat egg whites with salt and cream of tartar until they hold a point or will not fall out when tipped upside down. Next sprinkle the baking powder on whites and beat a little. Then pour very slowly, the heavy mixture into the rest, and fold in very carefully. Bake in a loaf or layer pan with heat as for other cake.

Yellow Angel Food

3 egg yolks
1 cup sugar
7 tbsp. cold water
1 tsp. vanilla
1 cup cake flour
1 tsp. baking powder
Pinch of salt
3 egg whites

Beat the egg yolks until lemon-colored. Add sugar and beat until good and light. Add cold water and vanilla and beat again. Sift flour, baking powder and salt together and add to batter. Beat well. Beat egg whites stiff and fold in lightly. Bake in a moderate oven.

SPONGE CAKES

Angel Sponge Cake

4 eggs
2 cups sugar
1 cup boiling water
2 cups cake flour
2 tsp. baking powder
½ tsp. cream of tartar

Beat eggs for 5 minutes, add sugar and beat thoroughly. Add the boiling water, then the flour containing baking powder and cream of tartar. Flavor to suit taste and bake in an ungreased pan about 40 minutes. This makes a large cake.

Hot Milk Sponge Cake

2 eggs
¼ tsp. salt
1 cup sugar
¼ tsp. almond flavoring
1 tsp. vanilla
1 tbsp. butter
½ cup boiling hot milk
1 cup sifted Gold Medal Flour
1 tsp. baking powder

Beat eggs and salt until very light. Beat in sugar and flavoring. Add butter to boiling milk and then add flour sifted with baking powder. Bake at once in an 8-inch square pan for 25 minutes at 325 degrees. Cut in strips. Roll in powdered sugar. This should be made with an electric mixer.

Speedy Sponge Cake

2 eggs
1 cup sugar
1 cup enriched flour
⅛ tsp. salt
1 tsp. baking powder
1 tbsp. butter
½ cup hot milk

Beat eggs until light and thick. Slowly add sugar and beat with a spoon 5 minutes or with an electric mixer for 2½ minutes. Fold sifted dry ingredients into egg and sugar mixture all at once. Melt butter in hot milk and add all at once. The folding-in of the dry ingredients and milk should take only 1 minute. Bake in a waxed paper-lined 8-inch square pan in a moderate oven (350 degrees) for 30 minutes.

Baked-On Frosting

Beat 1 egg white with ¼ tsp. baking powder. Gradually beat in ½ cup brown sugar and spread over hot cake. Sprinkle with ¼ cup chopped nutmeats. Bake in a moderate oven (350 degrees) until lightly browned and bubbly (about 15 minutes).

Orange Sponge Cake

5 eggs, divided
½ tsp. cream of tartar
1½ cups sugar (sifted)
3 tsp. grated orange rind
1¾ cups cake flour
2¼ tsp. baking powder
½ tsp. salt
½ cup orange juice

Beat egg whites and cream of tartar until stiff. Add well-beaten egg yolks, sugar and orange rind. Add flour sifted with baking powder and salt, and orange juice. Bake in 3 (8-inch) layer pans. Fill with rich lemon filling and frost with 3-minute frosting.

Sponge Cake

10 egg yolks
1 cup sugar
½ cup cold water
1½ cups cake flour
⅛ tsp. salt
1 tsp. baking powder
1 tsp. lemon extract

Place egg yolks, sugar and water in mixer and beat for 15 minutes at medium speed. Then sift the cake flour 4 times with the salt and baking powder. Fold into egg yolk mixture and add lemon extract. Bake 1 hour at 325 degrees.

Whipped Cream Cake

1 cup sweet cream
3 egg whites
½ cup water
1 tsp. vanilla
2 cups cake flour
3 tsp. baking powder
½ tsp. salt
1½ cups sugar

Whip cream after measuring. Beat egg whites until stiff and combine with cream. Add water and vanilla. Sift together flour, baking powder, salt and sugar (flour and sugar having been sifted separately several times). Gradually fold in dry ingredients into egg mixture a little at a time. Bake at 375 degrees for 30 minutes in a 9-inch layer pan.

Svea Johnson's Ugly Cake

History: Mrs. Johnson was an elderly widow, who made this delicious cake from apples her tree bore every fall. Though it was not expected of her, she always wanted to do her part in providing for the church suppers, so she brought her "Comfort Cake". Since it was not frosted, it was relegated to a position in the back at the end of the serving table. That is where we young ones discovered it, laid claim and enjoyed two or three helpings. It was quietly referred to by the committee, as "Mrs. Johnson's Ugly Cake". We watched for that cake and had little competition because it was so unassuming.

One year, a committee member told Mrs. Johnson she would come by and pick up the cake to make it easier for her; which she did. She took it home and covered it with a sour cream icing; then the cake became acceptable, others learned of the taste and we lost our claim to "Mrs. Johnson's Ugly Cake".

We paid a visit to Mrs. Johnson and asked for the recipe, which pleased her mightily. Whenever I make this cake, it brings back memories, and while the frosting is delicious, I never frost it, because it is so good in its unassuming state. (1930's)

Svea Johnson's Comfort Cake

2 cups sugar
3 cups flour
1 tsp. baking soda
1 tsp. salt
2 tsp. cinnamon

Mix above ingredients in a large bowl and then add:

1⅓ cup melted shortening
(I now use salad oil)
2 eggs
2 tsp. vanilla

Stir together and then add:

4 cups peeled, chopped apples
½ cup raisins

Pour batter in a greased 9x13 pan and bake for ½ hour at 325 degrees (her way) or 1 hour at 350 degrees (my way) until cake leaves the sides of the pan. The cake is moist and will keep for a long time if no one discovers it. If they do – it's a "flash in the pan".

Sour Cream Frosting

1 cup sour cream
1 cup sugar
3 or 4 egg yolks

Cook until thick, spread on cake and sprinkle with chopped nuts. (This is the frosting that spoiled our claim to the Ugly Cake and put it on the plates of the multitudes.)

FRUIT CAKES

Lovely to look at, lovely to behold,
Bought at bazaars, they're always marked sold.

Chock-full of citron, they're heavy as gold,
But no one will eat them is what we've been told.

Forsaken and lonely, they turn stale and old,
They sit on a shelf till they dry up and mold.

FRUITCAKES

Making and serving fruitcake at Christmas is not a unique Lutheran experience. In fact, Lutheran women rarely serve fruitcake at church functions. We are told that Christians from other cultures and religious persuasions are also caught up in this habit. "Why?" you ask. We can only guess. Maybe it's because some of the main ingredients found in fruitcakes – dates, nuts, citron and raisins, - remind Lutherans and other Christians of the Holy Lands. Maybe fruitcakes are something Lutherans and other Christians know they'll always have on hand just in case they're caught shorthanded without much to serve if someone drops by to visit; or maybe it's just a tradition that all Christians have learned to respect, but never question. Consequently, we felt a Lutheran obligation to put fruitcake recipes in this church cookbook.

Dark Fruitcake

1 lb. butter
1 lb. sugar
12 eggs
1 lb. flour
3 tbsp. grated nutmeg
1½ tbsp. cinnamon
1 tbsp. mace
2 lbs. raisins, chopped
2 lbs. currants, washed & dried
1 lb. citron, cut up
*1 lg. tumbler wine or fruit juice

Beat butter and sugar to a cream. Beat eggs without separating until light and creamy. Add to butter and sugar and mix in flour, with which spices have been sifted. Cut, wash and dry fruit and dredge with ½ cup flour and stir into cake. Take an extra large tumbler of wine or fruit juice and stir into cake last. Turn mixture into a well-greased pan and bake 3 hours – 250 degrees F. I like to steam this cake 3 hours and then bake it 1½ hours at 250 degrees F.

Don't use wine if there is a chance you might be bringing this to church.

Fruitcake

¾ cup Crisco or butter
1 cup sugar
4 eggs
3 cups sifted flour
1 tsp. soda
1 tsp. salt
½ tsp. cloves
½ tsp. cinnamon
½ tsp. allspice
¼ cup jelly
½ cup molasses
½ cup fruit juice or sour milk
1 cup nuts
½ lb. chopped dates
1 lb. currants
¼ lb. candied lemon peel
¼ lb. candied orange peel
¼ lb. citron
¼ lb. candied pineapple
¼ lb. candied red cherries
¼ lb. candied green cherries

Cream shortening and sugar and add eggs one at a time, beating well after each egg is added. Sift together the flour, soda, salt and spices, and add alternately with jelly, molasses and fruit juice or sour milk (all blended together). Add the nuts and chopped fruits that have been slightly floured. This may be baked in one-pound (low style) coffee cans or in small loaf pans. If pans are lined with waxed paper, cake will keep fresh longer.

Mincemeat Fruitcake

1 lb. mince meat
1 cup raisins
1 cup chopped nuts
1 cup chopped glazed fruit
½ cup melted shortening
1 cup sugar
2 eggs, separated
2 cups all-purpose flour
1½ tsp. baking powder
½ tsp. soda
1 tsp. salt
1 tsp. vanilla

To the mincemeat, add raisins, nutmeats and chopped fruit. Cream sugar and shortening, add egg yolks and beat thoroughly. Sift flour, baking powder, soda and salt together once, and then sift and fold into mincemeat mixture. Fold in stiffly beaten egg whites and vanilla. Grease pan well. Bake in a tube pan for 1½ hours.

Steamed Fruitcake

2 cups shortening
2⅔ cups lt. brown sugar
9 eggs
½ cup molasses
½ cup strong coffee infusion
½ cup grape or fruit juice
1 tbsp. vanilla
½ tsp. soda
5½ cups all-purpose flour
3 tsp. baking powder
1 tbsp. cloves
2 tbsp. cinnamon
1 tbsp. nutmeg
1 tsp. salt
2 lbs. raisins, chopped
1½ lbs. currants
½ lb. candied cherries
¼ lb. citron, cut fine
¼ lb. lemon peel, cut fine
¼ lb. orange peel, cut fine
2 cups almonds, blanched & chopped

Cream the shortening and sugar together. Beat the eggs and add, stirring until well mixed. Add the molasses, coffee, fruit juice, and vanilla. Dissolve the soda in a tablespoonful of hot water in the coffee and add to the mixture and stir. Sift the flour. Measure the correct amount, reserving 1 cup for dredging the fruit, and sift the remaining flour with the baking powder, spices and salt. Add the flour to the above mixture and beat. Add the fruit and almonds, dredged with flour, and stir until thoroughly mixed. Pour into 2 large or several small loaf pans lined with waxed paper. Whole almonds and candied cherries may be arranged on the tops of the cakes. Place in a steamer and steam 3 hours. Remove to a slow oven (300 degrees) and bake for 1 hour. Cool and store to ripen.

White Fruitcake

1 cup butter
2 cups sugar
1 cup sweet milk
1 bottle cherries with juice
4 cups flour
3 tsp. baking powder
1 cup coconut
1 cup nuts
½ cup each: citron, orange & lemon peel
1 lg. cup white raisins
1 lg. cup dates, cut up
1 tsp. vanilla
Pinch of salt
6 egg whites

Cream sugar and butter. Add milk and cherry juice alternately with sifted dry ingredients with the exception of 1 cup flour used to flour fruits and nuts. Add these after the milk and flour. Add extract and salt. Fold in stiffly beaten whites last. Bake 1 hour.

This one looks Norwegian!

LUTHERAN CHURCH BASEMENT WOMEN

LUTHERAN CHURCH BASEMENT WOMEN

TWENTY STATEMENTS THAT LUTHERAN WOMEN CAN'T SAY, BUT AT THE WRONG TIME OF THE MONTH, MIGHT THINK (Not Christian)

1. That's the fourth time she has used that excuse.
2. They are dying like flies around here. If I have to bring another cake, I think I will scream.
3. Don't call me for anything. I'm too busy.
4. Get some of the younger ones to do it.
5. If we run out, that's just too bad.
6. I don't want to listen to your complaints. I have enough trouble of my own.
7. Tell her to cater it!
8. It's about time we started using paper cups.
9. She hasn't been in church for ages, and then shows up for the banquet. Figures.
10. I don't know how she dares to ask us to serve.
11. We're not a restaurant for crying out loud.
12. I can't work. (no explanation).
13. Who does she think she is anyway?
14. What do we have a janitor for anyway?
15. I haven't seen the pastor's wife get her hands in a sink of water.
16. Nobody needs a big meal for a 3 o'clock funeral, that's for sure. Sandwiches will just have to do.
17. Life's not a bowl of cherries for anyone.
18. She isn't the only one who has got other commitments.
19. Let's keep it simple.
20. Why do Lutherans think they have to eat every time they go to church?

TWENTY STATEMENTS HEARD BY PROPER, CHEERFUL LUTHERAN WOMEN (Christian)

1. It's nothing
2. I'm sorry.
3. You sit down and let me do it.
4. I will be more than happy to help.
5. What can I bring then?
6. Don't think a thing about it.
7. I'll stand. I've been sitting all morning.
8. *Mange tusen tak.*
9. Give me the dishtowel. It's my turn now.
10. You've had a long day. Sit down then.
11. I haven't had my turn.
12. I have nothing better to do.
13. I can easily double the recipe.
14. It's *ingenting.*
15. Keep the dishes coming.
16. Give me the dishtowels. I'm washing tomorrow anyway.
17. I'm not helpless.
18. I can be there by 6 in the morning.
19. It's about time I return the favor.
20. Keep me posted. I can get there in a flash.

TYPES OF LUTHERAN CHURCH BASEMENT WOMEN

Mary types – The Listeners	Martha Types – The Doers
1. Gives devotions	1. Organizes kitchen crew
2. Serves coffee	2. Makes coffee
3. Arranges centerpiece	3. Sets and cleans tables
4. High heel shoes and nylons	4. Wedges and anklets
5. Fancy apron	5. Everyday or catchall apron
6. Introduces speaker	6. Serves speaker
7. Plays piano	7. Dusts piano
8. Visits with speaker	8. Washes dishes
9. Arranges for next speaker	9. Takes down tables & cleans
10. Announces meeting	10. Serves next meeting

LUTHERAN LADIES AID ETIQUETTE

1. Be a cheerful giver. Give food, money and time whenever called upon.
2. Be an officer. Even if you are shy, there's something you can do.
3. When the Ladies Aid president calls for a cake for a funeral, don't be skimpy. Use your biggest pan. Remember, funeral cake is cut into 4-inch squares.
4. If someone gives you a compliment on the food you prepared, a proper response would be – "It wasn't much then". Keep it humble and nobody will think you are a show-off.

5. Always bring more food than what is asked of you, so other people won't think you are cheap and skimpy.

TIMES TO BRING FOOD TO THE PASTOR

1. Day of arrival.
2. Christmas – bring your Sunday best. (Mark down the cost. This can be counted towards your tithe.)
3. When someone in the pastor's family is sick.
4. When the pastor's wife has a baby.
5. Easter.
6. When the pastor leaves – if he leaves in good standing.

LUTHERAN MEASUREMENTS – RULES OF THUMB

Time – Cook until done. It's just got that certain look.

A Little Bit – A couple of pinches, but go easy then.

Pinch – Not too much. (Wash hands before you do this.)

A lot – Make sure you have enough flour for this one.

Flour To Roll – Don't run out of flour. It could get to be a sticky situation.

Ingenting – A little less than ½ pinch. If you don't have the ingredient, it won't matter anyway.

Lunch For A Bunch - Always count on extras; you just never know. It is better to have enough than to run out.

Temperature Tester – Spit will sizzle when the pan is hot enough.

Recipe Stretching – Add water or flour depending upon the situation.

If no baking temperature is given, 350 degrees is as reliable as the noon whistle.

WOMEN'S APRONS

The Basic Six

1. **Serving Apron**

   This is the "Lutheran Standard" of all aprons. Most Lutheran women who are willing workers and willing servers own several of these 24-inch long, slightly pressed, gathered and tied at the waist, flowered or gingham-checked, cotton serving aprons. Adorned with only one handy pocket, these aprons are not used for heavy-duty serving.

2. **Anniversary Apron**

   Lutheran women who serve Silver and Golden Wedding Anniversaries in the church basement wear this apron. Most people who aren't Lutheran can't tell the difference between this apron and a serving apron. Lutheran women can. The anniversary apron is usually fancier. The gingham-checked aprons usually have some cross-stitch running across the bottom of the apron, and the flowered ones have a couple of rows of rickrack or trim on them to dress them up a little bit.

3. **Wedding Apron**

Lutheran brides purchase these little, white, lacy and see-through (not risqué though), stiff, organza aprons for friends and family members who serve coffee at their wedding. Given as a gift to the wedding coffee servers, they're usually put in a closet and never used again. They're impractical and a waste of good money, but they are necessary and appropriate attire for coffee servers at Lutheran weddings.

4. **Catch-All Apron**

Because they cover Lutheran servers from the shoulders to the knees, this all-purpose, understated apron is a favorite for Lutheran women when they're "heavy-duty" serving. (Heavy-duty serving takes place at annual lutefisk suppers.) Some Lutheran men* wear them when they're cooking for mother-daughter banquets. Loaded with pockets, they're practical but not pretty. In Lutheran homes these aprons are usually hung up and not folded in drawers.

*Lutheran men wear only white aprons.

5. **The Everyday Apron**

(Some pronounce it everday.) These are the worn-out serving and catch-all aprons that Lutheran women wear around their homes and only wear in church when they're doing the annual spring and fall cleaning of the church basement kitchen.

6. **Dishtowel Apron**

Another apron worn by both Lutheran women and Lutheran men is the dishtowel apron. Lutheran women wear them in a pinch when for some reason or another they forget their appropriate apron at home; but Lutheran men who do dishes at mother-daughter banquets use them without thinking a thing about it. Some Lutherans throw them over their shoulder when cooking so they have something to wipe their hands on, or they use them as potholders when the unexpected comes up.

Footnote: The young Mrs. Ole Johnson doesn't always get her wash done on Mondays, and her neighbor said she's seen her use a dishtowel as a diaper. Ish da. Then others said they weren't surprised because the mother of the young Mrs. Ole Johnson once wore a dishtowel over her head to church, took it off, and went into the church kitchen and started drying dishes with it. People talked about it for years and years. As Lena Larson said, "Train up a child . . .".

SAFE AND PROPER KNOTS USED FOR TYING LUTHERAN CHURCH BASEMENT WOMEN'S DISHTOWELS

For Aprons

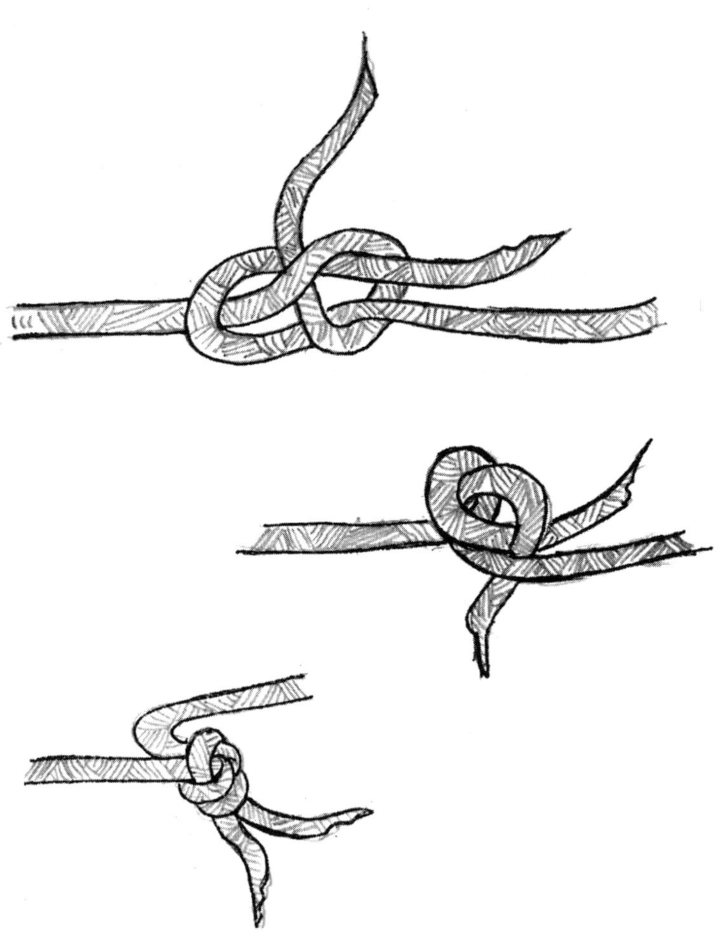

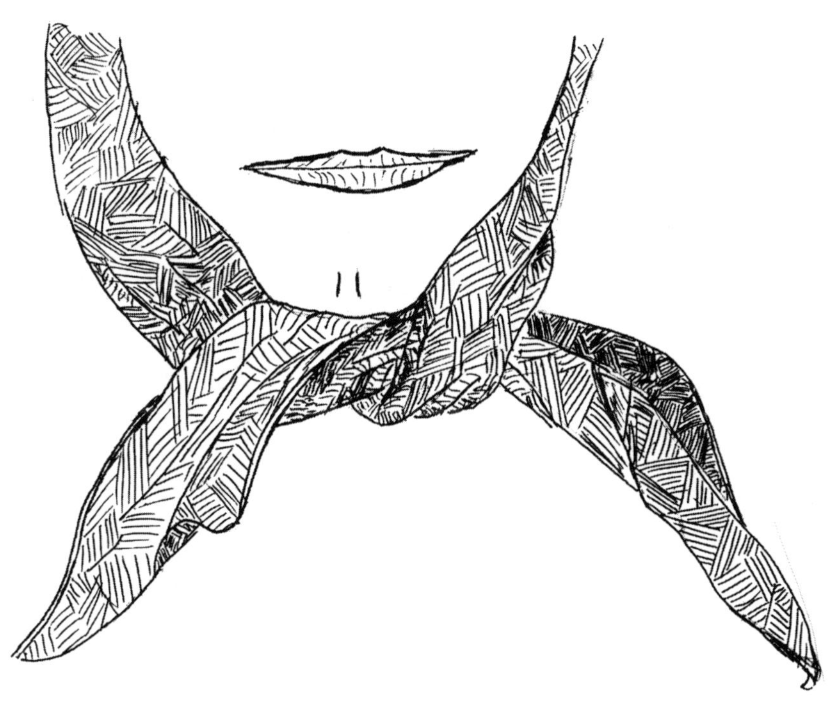

BETWEEN THE NINE AND ELEVEN

BETWEEN THE NINE AND ELEVEN

Non-Lutherans, heathens, and liberal psychologists are puzzled why Lutherans have to be served a little lunch between the 9 and 11 o'clock services. Some argue it's heredity, others say it's environmental, and the cynics say it's just a habit.

Ole Axelson, a baptized and confirmed Lutheran can't understand what the fuss is all about. "That's nothing to get excited about", he said. "The mind hears the words '*vær sa god*', and the stomach says it's time for lunch. It's as easy as that." Lena, his wife, says it's Biblical. "Jesus stopped his services so his disciples could gather fish and bread for everyone to eat. If it was good enough for the Lord, it's good enough for me", she said.

Coffee For Sixty

1 lb. coffee
12 quarts water

Put coffee into cloth bag large enough so that the coffee after swelling will be held loosely in the bag. Drop bag into boiling water. Boil for 5 to 8 minutes, then remove bag.
One quart of cream will serve 60 people.

Some made egg coffee depending upon who was serving.

Watkins Nectar and Kool-Aid

This was for the kids or visitors who didn't drink coffee. Sometimes only water was served.

Brown Sugar Cookies

1⅓ cups brown sugar
⅔ cup butter and lard
(in equal parts)
2 eggs
3 cups flour (rounding)
1 tsp. soda
2 tsp. cream of tartar
¼ tsp. salt
1 tsp. vanilla

Combine sugar, butter and eggs until well beaten. Add flour, soda, cream of tartar and salt, mixed and sifted together, and then vanilla. Roll thin and shape with a small cutter. Bake in a hot oven.

Three cups of flour is certainly different than three cups of flour (rounding). Lutheran Church Basement Women know the difference. Do you?

Butter Cookies

1 cup butter
1 cup granulated sugar
2 eggs
½ tsp. Watkins Lemon Extract
½ tsp. Watkins Vanilla
2¼ cups flour, sifted
1 tsp. Watkins Cream of Tartar
½ tsp. soda

Cream butter, add sugar and beat well. Add beaten eggs and flavorings and then the sifted dry ingredients. Chill dough. Roll thin on lightly floured board. Cut, sprinkle with sugar and decorate with bits of candied cherries. Bake on greased cookie sheet 8 to 10 minutes at 375 degrees F. Keep in covered tin. The less flour used, the more crisp the cookies.

Some cooks cheapen this cookie up by using lard. No one will say anything but everyone will know it. What could be worse then?

Excellent White Cookies

½ cup butter
½ cup lard
2 cups sugar
3 eggs, separated
½ tsp. baking powder
1 tsp. soda
Flour to mix for rolling
½ cup sweet milk

Beat shortening, add sugar and yolks and beat well. Add baking powder and soda to part of the flour. Add milk, whites of eggs and remaining flour. Roll out the dough very thin. Bake in a quick oven.

This recipe states that the cookies should be baked in a "quick oven". Only veteran cooks should try this recipe because they're the only ones who know what it means to bake cookies in a "quick oven".

Molasses Cookies

¾ cup shortening
1 cup white sugar
1 egg, beaten
4 tbsp. molasses
2 tsp. soda
¼ tsp. salt
2 cups flour and 2 or 3 tbsp. more if necessary
1 tsp. ginger
1 tsp. cinnamon
½ tsp. cloves

Mix and form in balls. Roll in sugar and bake.

This recipe calls for 2 cups of flour and 2 or 3 tablespoons more if necessary. Beware of this recipe if you don't have enough cooking sense to know how to feel dough.

Peanut Butter Cookies

1 cup brown sugar
½ cup butter
½ cup peanut butter
1½ cups flour
1 tsp. soda
Vanilla
Pinch of salt

Mix ingredients in the order given. Form in small balls on cookie sheet and press down with fork. Bake in oven at 350 degrees.

Not a dunker, but a hit with kids. Sometimes they get dry and stick to the roof of your mouth. Don't eat it if you have a habit of gagging or a condition that causes you to clear your throat.

Salted Peanut Cookies

1 cup butter, melted
2 cups brown sugar
2 eggs, well beaten
2 cups flour
1 tsp. baking powder
1 tsp. soda
1 cup oatmeal
1 cup Wheaties
1 cup salted peanuts (whole)

Cream shortening and sugar. Add well-beaten eggs. Next, add sifted flour, baking powder and soda. Then add the oatmeal, Wheaties and salted peanuts.

This is a hearty cookie. The "bread and butter stick-to-the-ribs type". This goes better in the winter.

Soft Ginger Cookies

1 cup brown sugar
¾ cup shortening
1 cup sour cream
1 cup molasses
½ tsp each: nutmeg, allspice, cloves and cinnamon
2 tsp. ginger
½ tsp. soda
1 heaping tsp. baking powder
½ tsp. salt
Flour to make soft dough

ICING

1 cup sugar
1 egg white, beaten
4 tbsp. boiling water
Flavoring

Boil.

Note: Since baking time is not included, a new bride shouldn't try this recipe.

Sugar Cookies

3 cups flour
1 tsp. baking powder
½ tsp. salt
1¼ cups sugar
1 cup shortening
3 eggs, beaten
1 tsp. vanilla
1 tsp. lemon extract

Sift dry ingredients. Add shortening, beaten eggs, vanilla and lemon flavoring. Cool in refrigerator. Roll out and cut with cookie cutter. Bake on a greased cookie sheet for 10 minutes at 375 degrees.

These cookies make as good a dunker as a lard doughnut.

Sour Cream Sugar Cookies

¾ cup sugar
⅓ cup shortening
1 egg
¼ tsp. salt
Grated rind of 1 orange
1¼ cups flour
½ tsp. soda
½ tbsp. baking powder

Blend sugar and shortening. Add beaten egg, salt and orange rind. Add flour that has been sifted with the soda and baking powder. Roll out thin and cut with cookie cutter and bake on greased cookie sheet for 10 minutes at 375 degrees.

If you don't have oranges in the house, just skip the orange rind the recipe calls for – people aren't usually too fussy at lunch between the 9 and 11.

Dream Bars

½ cup butter
½ cup brown sugar
1 cup flour

Mix with fingertips and press mixture into 9x13 pan. Bake 10 to 12 minutes. Remove from oven. Spread following mixture on top of above:

2 eggs
1 cup brown sugar
½ tsp. salt
2 tbsp. flour
½ cup coconut
1 cup nutmeats
1 tsp. vanilla

Return to oven and bake about 20 minutes. Cut into squares.

If you've been in the barn, wash your hands before you bake these because this recipe calls for mixing the ingredients with your fingertips.

Honey Date Bars

2 eggs
1 cup honey
1 tsp. vanilla
1 cup chopped nuts

1⅓ cups flour
1 tsp. baking powder
1 lb. chopped dates

Beat the eggs and add honey, flour and baking powder. Beat well. Add vanilla, nuts and dates. Spread on 10x15 cookie sheet, ¼ inch deep. When baked, cut in strips ½ inch wide and 3 inches long. Roll in powdered sugar before serving. Bake at 375 degrees for 12 minutes.

Take heed about eating this bar if you wear plates. Some cooks get a little carried away with the dates, and these bars become a little bit too chewy!

Doughnuts

1 cup sugar
4 tbsp. lard, melted
2 eggs
½ tsp. salt
1 cup sour milk
1 tsp. soda
3 cups flour
1 tsp. cinnamon
½ tsp. nutmeg

Combine the sugar, lard, beaten eggs and salt. Add sour milk to which soda has been added. Mix in the flour, cinnamon and nutmeg thoroughly. Roll out to about ⅓ inch thick and cut with the doughnut cutter. Fry in deep fat until golden brown.

Good for dunking. Lard doughnuts are as Lutheran as apple pie is American.

Watkins Cocoa Frosting

2 heaping tbsp. Watkins Cocoa
1 cup confectioners' sugar
Pinch of salt
Watkins hot coffee to blend
¼ tsp. Watkins Vanilla

Mix Watkins Cocoa, sugar and salt. Add enough Watkins Coffee to make smooth paste. Add Watkins Vanilla and beat well. Put in bowl and they can frost their own doughnuts if they want to.

FUNERAL AND OTHER DEAD SPREADS

Bologna Filling

1½ cups ground bologna
2 hard-boiled eggs, finely chopped
4 tbsp. salad dressing
½ tsp. salt
A little bit of pepper

Smash together and put on bread or buns. Don't be stingy with bologna spread.

Braunschweiger Filling

½ lb. braunschweiger liver sausage
½ cup drained pickle relish
4-6 tbsp. salad dressing

Mix it all up and put on bread.

Not a favorite of children, but then they either ate it or went hungry. Missouri Synods felt welcome in the "other" Lutheran churches when this was served.

Cheese Spread

2 hard-cooked eggs, grated
1 sm. jar pimento, chopped
½ lb. grated American cheese
1 tbsp. chopped onion
Salt and pepper

A spread used on rye or wheat bread is a favorite for funerals when serving light and dark sandwiches.

Funeral Meat

A sandwich filling always used for lunches at funerals (used on buns or bread).

3 lbs. minced ham (ground)
Today it is known as bologna meat.

12 eggs, hard-boiled
1 pt. Kraft sandwich spread

Grind meat and hard-boiled eggs. Mix in the pint of sandwich spread. Enough for 1 dozen buns.

HAM OR SPAM, THE KING OF ALL SPREADS

Ham and Egg Sandwich

3 hard-boiled eggs, chopped
1 cup baked or boiled ground ham or spam
¾ cup homemade mixed pickle relish
¾ cup mayonnaise
1 tsp. chopped onion (if desired)

Mix together thoroughly and spread generously between slices of bread or opened faces. Also works well on open-faced buns.

Ingebrit's Egg Sandwich Spread

2 hard-cooked eggs
3 pimentos
½ lb. American cheese
1 sm. onion, minced
½ tsp. salt
Pepper

Chop the eggs; dice pimentos and cheese. Add onions, salt and pepper. Put together with this dressing:

1 tbsp. butter
1 tbsp. sugar
1 tbsp. flour
3 tbsp. vinegar
½ cup milk

Mix and boil until clear. Yields 2 cups.

Ingebrit said to go easy on the onion if serving at a funeral where the mourners are getting up there in age when spices don't sit so well.

OTHER SPREADS

Basic Egg Salad Filling

4 hard-cooked eggs, chopped fine
3 tbsp. chopped sweet pickle
3 tbsp. salad dressing
½ tsp. prepared mustard
¼ tsp. onion salt
Few grains pepper

This one gets the vote from the woman who needed a quick sandwich spread to serve for Luther League. It is usually served on wheat or white, or if you really want to jazz things up, you take one slice of white and one of wheat, put in the filling, cut the bread diagonally, and you would have yourself a two-toned sandwich.

Ladies Aid Supreme – Dried Beef on White

Butter white bread. Put on 1 or 2 thin layers of dried beef and watch the sandwiches disappear.

Chicken or Turkey Filling

1 cup minced cooked chicken
¼ cup finely chopped celery
1 tsp. minced parsley
3 tbsp. thick sour cream
¼ tsp. salt
little bit of pepper

Mix this all together and put on buns.

This was usually used for fancy occasions such as weddings, showers or anniversaries.

Deluxe Spread

Spread rye bread with Cheez Whiz. Lay the stuffed olives on their side like watermelon and cut into cute little rings. Place on rye bread in pattern and cut rye bread on the diagonal.

Pretty as a picture and easy to eat.

Novelty Sandwich Spread

American cheese on wheat
Thinly sliced radishes on homemade, buttered, whole wheat bread
Peanut butter and jelly
Summer sausage on white bread

These are not necessarily served in a church but sometimes you see something like this.

SANDWICH SECRETS

1. Use bread one day old.

2. Let butter stand one hour at room temperature and cream thoroughly; do not melt butter.

3. Use plenty of filling and spread to edge.

4. For thin sandwiches, spread loaf with creamed butter; then slice. Butter each slice of bread.

5. Lettuce keeps sandwich moist. Have lettuce crisp.

6. Do not have fillings too moist or too dry.

7. Toasted sandwiches should be spread with filling but no butter. Spread outside with melted butter and toast in oven.

8. The secret of good sandwiches is in having filling well seasoned. Use Watkins Pepper, Watkins Celery Salt, Watkins Onion Seasoning, Watkins Dry Mustard and Watkins Paprika.

FUNERAL PLATES

German Lutheran Funeral Plate

Bratwurst

Beans

Chips

Pickles

Cakes

Coffee

Scandinavian Lutheran Funeral Plate

Hotdish

Pickles

Jell-O

Cake

Coffee

CHURCH BASEMENT *LUTEFISK* FEEDS

If there were ever justification for second helpings, it was at the annual church basement *lutefisk* feeds. After reading the following list of foods needed for one of these huge undertakings, you will know why the red-armed, tired women who prepared this feast were hustled out of the kitchen for a heartfelt round of applause.

Lutefisk dinner for 1200
600 pounds of *lutefisk*
400 pounds of meatballs
116 pounds of butter
600 pounds of potatoes
276 cans of corn
40 gallons of coleslaw
40 quarts of dill pickles
20 quarts of beet pickles
600 pieces of *lefse*
20 loaves of rye bread (for the Swedes)
60 dozen buns
3,500 cups of coffee
Between 5,000-6,000 Scandinavian cookies such as *krum-kaka*, spritz, etc

Vær sa god!!!

FOOTNOTE: Our Scandinavian ancestors did not have the standard English measurements that we use today. Their recipes may have called for all kinds of odd measures:

> *barneskje* – child's spoon
> *teskje* – half a teaspoon
> *spiseskje* – one soup spoon
> *en smule* – a crumb of this or that
> *knap en liter* – not quite a liter

SALADS

Coleslaw Dressing

10 tbsp. sugar
1 tsp. dry mustard
1 tsp. salt
1 cup oil
1 cup grated onion

Beat the above together and add slowly:
½ cup vinegar
½ tsp. celery salt or celery seed and a trace of garlic

Pickled Beets

Wash beets thoroughly. Boil until tender. Remove skins and dice. To 5 quarts diced beets, add 5 cups of liquid in which beets were boiled, 1 cup vinegar, 1 cup sugar and 5 tsp. salt. Bring to boil; pour over beets and seal. Heat before serving, drain off liquid and add butter. For Harvard Beets, thicken the juice with a little cornstarch mixed with cold water and boil. Add vinegar and sugar to taste.

FLATBREADS

Flatbrød

1 cup graham flour
2 cups white flour
1 tsp. salt
1 tbsp. shortening
2 cups boiling water

Mix and let stand until cold. Add more flour and roll thin. Bake in oven on flat surface.

Knäckebröd II
(Hard Tack)

1 cup coarse rye meal
1 cup rye flour
1 tbsp. sugar
1½ tsp. salt
4 tbsp. butter
½ cup milk

Lutefisk Grøt
(*Lutefisk* Pudding)

1 cup rice
1 quart milk
2 eggs, beaten
2 tbsp. butter
1 tsp. salt
1 tsp. sugar
Dash of nutmeg
Cooked *lutefisk*

METHOD: Scald rice, then cook in milk until thick. Add rest of ingredients and pour into a buttered baking dish. Add a little more scalded milk if necessary. Sprinkle with buttered bread crumbs and bake in moderate oven about 1 hour. This is a good way to use leftover *lutefisk*. Other cooked fish such as pike, pickerel, salmon, etc. may also be used.

Lutefisk Pudding

¾ cup rice
2 cups cooked *lutefisk*
2 eggs, beaten
2 cups thin cream
Butter
Salt and pepper to taste

Cook rice in salted boiling water. Mix rice and *lutefisk* together; add eggs, cream, butter, salt and pepper. Bake in buttered baking dish, and serve with drawn butter. (A good way to serve leftover *lutefisk*.)

Potato *Lefse*

5 cups mashed potatoes
1½ cups flour
2 tbsp. melted butter
1 tsp. salt
1 tsp. sugar

Cook potatoes and mash the day before. Mash again before measuring. Makes 12 medium rounds.

Hardanger *Lefse*

2 eggs
½ tsp. soda
Pinch of salt
1½ tsp. ground cardamom (optional)
2 cups sour cream
½ cup sugar
3¾ cups flour to roll

Put in refrigerator overnight. Go easy on flour as you can always add more. Take a teaspoon and roll out in flour like flatbread. Fry on a pancake griddle a bit on both sides. Store in big container. To serve, put between damp towels to moisten so they are soft. Then spread with butter, sugar and cinnamon. Fold over and cut in wedges to serve. A very old recipe.

Lefse

18 potatoes
2 tsp. lard
1 tsp. salt
Flour

Boil and mash or rice potatoes. Cool. Add lard, salt and flour, a little at a time until dough can be rolled out easily. Roll as thin as possible. Bake on top of stove or on pancake griddle until a light brown, turning frequently to prevent scorching. Use moderate heat.

Lefse

5 large potatoes
½ cup sweet cream
3 tbsp. butter
1 tsp. salt
Flour – use ½ cup flour to each cup of mashed potatoes.

METHOD: Boil potatoes, mash very fine and add cream, butter and salt; beat until light and then let cool. Add flour and roll into a ball, kneading until smooth. Form into a long roll and slice in pieces about the size of a large egg, or larger, depending on the size of *lefse* desired. Roll each piece round as for pie crust and as thin as possible. Bake on *lefse* griddle or pancake griddle until light brown, turning frequently so as not to scorch. Use moderate heat. Do not grease the pan. When baked, place between clean cloths or waxed paper to keep them from becoming dry. Serve cold with butter, sugar and cinnamon. Cut each *lefse* in halves or fourths and roll up before serving.

Lefse

4 large potatoes, boil and mash; add 4 tbsp. shortening and 6 tbsp. cream. While still hot, add flour to make dough that can be rolled out thin. Chill. Bake on pancake griddle until brown on both sides. Use spatula for turning pieces. Makes 12.

Lefse

4 cups riced potatoes
1 tsp. salt
¼ cup shortening
¼ cup very rich cream (creamery)
1¼ cups flour

Cook potatoes and rice while hot. Add salt, shortening, and cream. Cool. Just before you roll your lefse, add the flour. A pastry cloth and sleeve work well when you roll it out. Makes 10 to 12.

Lutefisk

Soak *lutefisk* in cold water for 3-4 hours before using. Remove dark skin and fins, and cut in serving size pieces. Place in cheesecloth and put on to boil in a kettle of cold water, to which salt has been added. Cook about 5 minutes until fish is tender, then drain and serve with drawn butter or a cream sauce.

VARIATION: Try a little prepared mustard with *lutefisk* and butter.

Lutefisk

Cut off head and tail from fish and then cut fish into 4-inch lengths. Soak in mild saltwater overnight. In the morning, soak in clear, cold water for 5 hours. Drain well. Put fish into cheesecloth bags or sugar sacks, filling bags half full. Drop fish bags into boiling, salted water and boil for five minutes. Remove bags from water and drain. Skin and bone fish with a spoon. Keep fish warm in a large bowl or crock until ready to serve. Serve with melted butter.

White Sauce for *Lutefisk*

2 tbsp. butter
2 tbsp. flour
¼ tsp. salt
1 cup milk
Dash of pepper

METHOD: Make a white sauce and add seasonings to taste. For variation, add a teaspoon of prepared mustard to sauce.

Meatballs

For meatballs, mince two pounds of round,
Then add a pound of pork steak, ground.
A cup of "taters", then you mash
And beat two eggs into this hash.
One cup of bread crumbs, all dried up,
Some fresh sweet milk, about a cup.
Two teaspoons use to salt it down,
And one of sugar – best if brown.
Half teaspoons each of ginger, cloves,
And allspice in the mix now goes;
Nutmeg and pepper add to taste,
Then stir till mixture is a paste.
Now form in balls, and roll in flour,
And fry them well for half an hour.
Add cream, one pint, then let them bake,
Which forty minutes more will take.

Swedish Meatballs

4 lb. ground beef
3 beaten eggs
2 cups cold water or milk if you prefer
½ tsp. allspice
¼ cup onion
2 lb. lean pork
2 cups dry bread crumbs
3 tsp. salt (1 tsp. to 1 lb. meat)
1 tsp. pepper

Makes about 40 balls.

This recipe was used for lutefisk suppers and smorgasbords. It was Nettie Sathers recipe from Hauges.

Kjøtkaker (Norwegian Meatballs)

2½ lbs. ground round steak
½ cup suet
1 egg
1 cup cream
½ onion, minced
2½ tsp. salt
¼ tsp. pepper
⅛ tsp. nutmeg
1 tsp. baking powder

Grind meat and suet very fine. Beat egg slightly. Boil and cool cream. Mince onion fine. Add egg, cream, onion, seasonings and baking powder to meat and beat thoroughly until very light. Form into small balls, brown in butter and steam in gravy.

Kottbullar (Swedish Meatballs)

3 lbs. ground beef
1 quart cream
2 tsp. salt
¼ tsp. pepper
¼ tsp. allspice
1 cup bread crumbs

Grind beef very fine, add cream and beat thoroughly. Add seasonings and bread crumbs. (Rice Krispies or Corn Flakes, crushed fine, may be substituted for bread crumbs). Mix with beater until light. Form into small balls, brown in butter and make gravy from drippings, and simmer meatballs therein.

Swedish Meatballs in Gravy

10 slices white bread
4 eggs, beaten
½ tsp. white pepper
½ tsp. nutmeg
½ cup minced onion
1 tsp. Worcestershire Sauce
3 lbs. ground meat
3 tsp. salt
2 tbsp. lemon juice
½ tsp. paprika
cup chopped parsley

Soak bread in water to cover; squeeze out. Add beaten eggs to bread and remaining ingredients. Mix thoroughly with fingers. Form into 32 balls about 1½ inch in diameter; do not press hard. Roll in seasoned flour. Brown balls on all sides in ½ cup hot fat in Dutch oven. Mix ½ cup flour with 1 cup chicken stock or bouillon and 3 cups more liquid and pour over meatballs. Reduce heat and simmer 50 minutes. If gravy is too thin, thicken with a small amount of flour and water. Serves 16

POTATOES

Some Boil
Some Mash
Some Rice
But only russets will suffice!

COOKIES AND GOODIES
SØTSUPPE AND *GRØT*

Berlinerkranser

1 hard-boiled egg yolk
½ cup sugar
2 raw egg yolks (beat)
1 cup butter
3 cups flour

Mash boiled yolk with the sugar. Add the rest of ingredients. Roll with fingers to pencil size. Loop. Dip in beaten egg whites and then in sugar – preferably crushed loaf sugar. Bake at 350 degrees until slightly browned.

Fattigmann

12 egg yolks
½ cup sugar
1 cup whipping cream
3¾ cups flour

Beat egg yolks alone for 20 minutes; then with sugar for 15 minutes. Add cream, whipped, and flour a little at a time, leaving some of the flour for rolling. Let stand overnight in a cool place. Roll out and fry in deep fat.

Klejner-Fattigmand (Danish)

1 cup sugar
½ cup butter
2 eggs
6 tbsp. sweet cream
1 tsp. vanilla
1 tsp. baking powder
Flour enough to make a soft dough

Roll ¼ inch thick and cut in strips 1½ by 4 inches. Cut slit in each and put end through to form a twist. Fry in deep fat till light brown.

Kringle

6 cups flour
1 tsp. soda
1 tsp. baking powder
¼ tsp. nutmeg
1 cup sugar
1 cup sweet cream
1 cup buttermilk

Sift flour, soda, baking powder and nutmeg together. Add sugar, cream and buttermilk gradually, mixing well. Roll out on floured board or cloth and cut into ¼ inch strips about 4 inches long. Form into *kringle* and bake on oiled cookie sheet for 20 minutes at 375 degrees.

Kringler (Danish)

4 cups flour
½ cup sugar
¼ tsp. salt
1 tsp. soda
1 cup butter
2 cups sour cream

Sift together flour, sugar, salt and soda. Cut butter into dry ingredients like pastry. Add cream and flour to make a soft dough to roll. Cut in strips ½ inch wide and 9 inches long. Form a figure 8. Dip in beaten egg white and sprinkle with sugar and bake at 400 degrees.

Krumkaker

Norwegian:	English:
1 egg	1 egg
1 kopp suker	1 cup sugar
1 kopp hvetemel	1 cup wheat flour
1 kopp potetmel	1 cup potato flour
1 kopp smør	1 cup butter
1 kopp vann	1 cup water

Mix well. Mixture is consistency of light pancake dough. Heat iron. Experiment with heat until you find the correct temperature for your iron. Place about a soup spoonful of the mixture on the hot iron. Bake about ½ minute on that side. Turn the iron over and bake other side about ½ minute. A spatula is helpful in removing it. Roll on cylinder. When slightly cool, remove it.

Krumkaker

6 eggs
1 cup sugar
1 cup butter
2 cups flour

Beat eggs until light, adding sugar gradually. Add melted butter and flour, a little at a time. Bake on iron and roll quickly; or form into patty shells, fill with fruit and top with whipped cream.

Mousies or Snowballs

1 cup butter
½ cup confectioners sugar
2¼ cups sifted flour
¼ tsp. salt
1 tsp. vanilla
¾ cup finely chopped nuts

Mix in order given and form into small balls. Bake at 400 degrees for 15 minutes. While still hot, roll in powdered sugar. Let cool and roll in powdered sugar again.

Norwegian Butter Cookies

¾ cup butter
½ cup sugar
1 egg
1 tsp. vanilla
1 tsp. baking powder
1 cup flour
¾ cup cornstarch

Melt butter and cool until lukewarm. Add sugar and beat well. Add well-beaten egg, vanilla and dry ingredients sifted together. Drop by spoonfuls 2 or 3 inches apart. Bake 16 to 18 minutes at 350 degrees.

B. G. Rosettes

2 eggs, well-beaten
1 tsp. sugar
¼ tsp. salt
1 cup milk
1 cup flour

Heat lard or other cooking fat to 375 degrees. Let rosette iron heat in fat before dipping into dough. Shake off excess fat. When you dip iron into dough be very careful to avoid getting dough on top of iron. If dough does not adhere to iron, the iron may be too cold or have too much fat on it.

Bake in hot fat, 375 degrees, until light brown. Ease rosette off iron onto an absorbent towel. Makes about 40.

Rosettes

2 eggs
1 tsp. sugar
1 cup sweet milk
1 cup flour

Beat eggs lightly, add sugar, milk and flour, mixing until smooth. Fry in deep fat on rosette iron, cooling the iron each time while sugaring the rosette just baked. Having the iron too warm makes the rosettes greasy.

Sandbakkels

1 cup butter
1 cup sugar
2 cups flour
1 egg
½ cup finely chopped blanched almonds

Cream butter and sugar and add flour a little at a time. Add egg and almonds. Press into tins and bake at 350 degrees.

Sprits

½ cup butter
1 cup brown sugar
1 egg
1 tsp. soda
2 cups flour
½ tsp. cream of tartar
1 tsp. ginger
1 tsp. lemon extract

Cream butter and add sugar gradually. Add well-beaten egg and soda dissolved in warm water. Add flour, cream of tartar and ginger, sifted together. Add lemon extract. Put through cookie press.

Sprutbakkelse

1 cup butter
½ cup Crisco
1 cup sugar
1 egg, beaten
1 tsp. vanilla
½ tsp. salt
About 2 cups flour

Cream shortening and add sugar gradually. Add beaten egg and vanilla. Add flour and salt, mixing well. Put dough in cookie press and make cookies of various designs.

Strull

¾ cup sugar
1½ cups flour
Ground cardamom
1 cup whipping cream
½ cup half-and-half
½ cup whole milk

Mix sugar and flour well and add the cardamom. Add one cup whipping cream and stir until smooth. Add the half-and-half and the whole milk. Bake on heated *strull* iron on both sides until light brown. Roll on cone while hot. Makes about 4 dozen.

Rommegrøt

1 cup butter, melted
1 cup buttermilk, cold
1 cup flour, mixed smoothly

Bring to a boil.
3 cups cold milk
Salt (small amount)

Rommegrøt (Scandinavian)

1 quart whipping cream (at least 24 hours old)
1 cup flour
1 quart milk (boiled)
1 tbsp. sugar
1 tsp. salt

Using heavy kettle, boil cream 10 to 15 minutes. Add flour slowly using a wire whip to keep mixture smooth. Keep boiling on lower heat and stir until butter appears. Add boiled milk and boil and stir to right consistency. Add sugar and salt. Put into bowl and pour butter over. Sprinkle with sugar and cinnamon. Serve lukewarm.

Risengren (Rice Soup)

Cook rice. Add rich milk to make it soupy and a cinnamon stick. Cook slowly for an hour, stirring frequently. Serve with sugar.

Søtsuppe (Sweet Soup)

2 quarts water
½ cup sago
1 cup raisins
1 cup prunes
1 glass jelly or grape juice
1 cup sugar
2 sticks cinnamon
1 lemon
1 tbsp. vinegar

Wash sago, raisins and prunes. Cook sago, raisins and prunes in water for an hour. Add sugar, cinnamon, sliced lemon and vinegar. Boil again for thirty minutes; add jelly or grape juice about 15 minutes before soup is cooked.

Sweet Soup

2 lbs. prunes
½ cup currants
1½ cups raisins
1 lemon, peeled
1 cup pearl tapioca or sago
1½ cups sugar

Soak fruit overnight. Soak tapioca. Cook prunes, currants, raisins and lemon. Add tapioca and cook over low heat until tiny spots inside "pearls" show. Add sugar and cinnamon or cinnamon sticks.

Ham was served, and blessings were counted. At the end of the meal the offering plate was passed, and we were challenged to "give until it hurts". Some did. Others ate their ham, put in their dollar, and went home.

HARVEST FESTIVALS
(food placed as usually remembered on table)

Harvest Beets

¼ cup sugar
1-3 tbsp. cornstarch
¼ cup weak vinegar
1 cup diced beets (cooked)
1 tsp. butter

Mix sugar and corn starch; add the vinegar. Boil for 5 minutes. Pour over the diced beets; allow to stand over slow flame for about 15 to 20 minutes. Add butter before serving.

Buns

Soak 2 cakes compressed yeast in 1 cup cold water. In a large bowl, put 1 cup hot water, 1 cup shortening and ½ cup sugar. When cool, add yeast and water, 1¼ tsp. salt, 2 beaten eggs and 6½ cups flour. (Do not sift flour before measuring). Let rise, knead down and let rise again. Form into buns. Makes 48 buns.

Ham, Pineapple and Sweet Potato

1 (1-inch) ham slice
¼ tsp. cloves
¼ tsp. mustard
2 tbsp. brown sugar
1 (No. 2) can sliced pineapple
3 sweet potatoes

Place ham in pan and sprinkle with cloves, mustard and brown sugar. Cover with slices of pineapple. Cut sweet potatoes lengthwise, which have been cooked and peeled. Dip in fat and place around ham. Cover with pineapple juice to the depth of ½ inch and bake for 25 minutes at 375 degrees.

Scalloped Ham and Potatoes

2 (½-inch thick) slices of smoked ham
4 cups sliced raw potatoes
Salt
Pepper
Celery salt
Mustard
2 cups milk

Lay one slice ham in bottom of casserole. Cover with thinly sliced potatoes. Season with salt, pepper, celery salt and mustard. Lay second slice of ham on top. Pour milk over all. (If necessary, use more milk to completely cover.) Sprinkle with bread crumbs, dot with butter and bake at 375 degrees for 1 hour.

Carrot and Apple Casserole

3 cups sliced and cooked carrots
½ tsp. salt
1½ cups sliced tart apples
½ cup brown sugar
3 tbsp. butter
⅓ cup water

Put a layer of carrots in a greased casserole and sprinkle lightly with salt. Cover this with a layer of apples, sprinkled with sugar and dotted with butter. Repeat until carrots and apples are used up. Add the water. Cover closely and bake in a hot oven until apples are tender. Remove cover and allow to brown. Bake for 40 minutes at 375 degrees.

English Raisin Cake

1 lb. raisins
1½ cups sugar
½ cup butter
2 eggs
3 cups flour
2 tsp. soda
3 tsp. cinnamon
1 tsp. nutmeg
⅛ lb. citron
½ cup chopped nuts

Simmer raisins in water to cover, using 1 cup of the water in the cake. Cream sugar and butter. Add eggs, beating well. Add sifted dry ingredients alternately with the water. Add fruit and nuts. Mix thoroughly. Bake for 45 minutes at 375 degrees in a 9x13 pan.

Maple Nut Cake

⅓ cup shortening
1 cup light brown sugar
2 eggs, separated
¾ cup milk
1½ cups flour
½ tsp. salt
2 tsp. baking powder
1 cup nuts
1 tsp. vanilla

Cream shortening with brown sugar. Add egg yolks. Mix and add milk. Sift and add flour, salt and baking powder. Add nuts and vanilla. Fold in beaten egg whites. Bake 35 minutes at 325 degrees.

Watkins Economy Spice Cake
(Butterless, Eggless and Milkless)

1 cup brown sugar
1 cup boiling water
⅓ cup lard
1 cup raisins (more if desired)
1½ cups flour
1½ tsp. Watkins Baking Powder
¼ tsp. Watkins Nutmeg
1 tsp. Watkins Cinnamon
⅛ tsp. Watkins Cloves
¼ tsp. Watkins Ginger
¼ tsp. Watkins Allspice
½ tsp. salt
1½ tsp. Watkins Vanilla

Boil sugar, water, lard and raisins together about 3 minutes until sugar is well dissolved. Put aside until cool. Sift flour, Watkins Baking Powder and spices together. Add to above mixture and then add flavoring. Bake in a moderate oven. Use a small square tin.

Blood Bologna

2 cups blood
2 cups sour milk or buttermilk
2 cups sweet milk, can be used instead of buttermilk and soda
3 grated raw potatoes
3 cups white flour to 1 cup graham
½ tsp. soda
½ tsp. pepper
3 tbsp. salt
1 tbsp. allspice
2 cups leaf fat (cut in cubes)

Mix liquid, adding potatoes and sifting in dry ingredients. Stir in fat. Have sacks of muslin sewed 3x8 inches, filled ¾ full and tied well. Place in boiling water and cook 2 hours. If sweetening is desired, add some raisins or a little brown sugar.

Covered Wagon Cookies

2 qt. sorghum
1 pt. corn syrup
4 cups sugar
1 tbsp. salt
About 24 cups flour (in all)
1 tbsp. allspice
1 tbsp. cinnamon
1½ tsp. cloves
5 qt. black walnuts or 2 qt. walnuts and the rest pecans
4 tbsp. soda (dissolved in ¼ cup warm water)
1 cup sour cream

These cookies came with my grandmother on a covered wagon when she left Ladysmith, Wisconsin, to settle in Spring Valley. One batch makes a bushel of cookies and the older they get, the better they are. That is why they are called covered wagon cookies, as they came with many a wagon across the prairies. The longer they are kept, the chewier they become and the more flavorful.

Mix in a pan the sorghum, corn syrup and sugar. Cook these ingredients just to dissolve the sugar. Add 1 tbsp. of salt dissolved in a little water to this. Add 4 cups flour to this and place in a cool place, not the refrigerator.

The day before you want to start baking, set the pan in a warm place. Add cinnamon, allspice, cloves, walnuts and sour cream. Dissolve the 4 tbsp. soda in ¼ cup warm water and add to mixture. Knead well and gradually put in more flour. In all, this takes about 24 cups of flour. Four you have already mixed. See that 20 more cups get mixed in, including the cup or two that you might use when you roll them out. Roll at least ⅓ inch thick and cut about 1-inch wide and 3-inches long. You can cut shapes, but there are so many, you may wish to just use the bars. Bake each bar separately, however, not as bar cookies. 8 minutes at 350 degrees. Store in tight tin cans; don't freeze.

These are not sweet cookies. You can glaze them if you wish with 1 cup sugar and 1 cup water, cooked and cooled. We kept them from Thanksgiving to Thanksgiving.

Deviled Eggs

6 hard-boiled eggs
⅛ tsp. pepper
About 3 tbsp. salad dressing or cream
½ tsp. dry mustard
½ tsp. salt

After you cut the hard-boiled eggs in half, scoop out the yolks and mash the devil out of them. Stir in the rest of the ingredients and fill the hollowed out eggs with the egg yolk mixture.

A good thing to bring to a missionary picnic when time and money is a little tight. Fancy it up with a dash of paprika.

Easy Hotdish

1½ cups raw, cubed potatoes
1 can cream of celery soup
1½ cups cubed raw coarse balony (fancy people spell it bologna)

Mix and cover. Bake at 350 degrees for 45 minutes. The last few minutes put on strips of cheese. Serves 2

Only someone who didn't have kids would think of making a casserole that served only two.

Hamburger Hotdish

Brown 1 lb. hamburger with 1 small onion. Mix with 1 can cream of mushroom soup, 1 can cream of chicken soup and 1 can of cream style corn. Pour mixture over about 5 sliced potatoes in a large casserole. Bake 1 hour at 350 degrees.

Mrs. Benson said, "If you don't cook this long enough, it gets kind of soupy and hard to eat if it's on a thin paper plate.

Hamburger Rice Hotdish

Brown 1 lb. hamburger and 1 onion. Add 2 cans chicken gumbo, 1 can water and 1 cup raw rice. Bake in covered casserole for 1½ hours at 350 degrees. More liquid may be added, if needed. Keep it covered.

The late Mrs. Sven Hanson didn't keep it covered and her hamburger rice hotdishes were always dried out.

Hotdish

2 lbs. ground veal or beef
1 lb. ground salt pork
1 cup bread crumbs
2 eggs
2 tbsp. fat
1 cup diced celery
1 cup diced carrots
1 onion, diced
1 can tomato soup
1 can water

Mix ground meat, salt pork, bread crumbs and slightly beaten eggs. Form into meatballs and brown in the fat. Put in a baking dish. Mix celery, carrots, onion, tomato soup and water and pour over the meatballs. Bake for 1 hour at 325 degrees. This serves 10.

Most people wouldn't use veal at a Lutheran Church festival. Hamburger is sufficient.

Hotdish for 100

5 lbs. macaroni
5 lbs. ground beef
30 med onions, diced
¼ cup shortening
50 average size potatoes
3 cans green beans
3 (No. 2) cans corn
3 bunches celery
3 qts. tomatoes

Cook and drain macaroni. Brown meat and onion together in shortening. Dice potatoes and cook about 10 minutes. Some of the potato water may be saved to be used for moisture if needed. Mix all together and bake. Carrots may be added if desired or if you have to stretch it.

This is a good old stand-by for funerals, too. Especially funerals of members who are in good standing and well-liked by most.

Hungarian Goulash

2 tbsp. fat
1 lb. hamburger
1 small onion, if desired
1 cup chopped celery
2 cups cooked rice
1 (No. 1) can tomatoes
1 can kidney beans

Melt fat in frying pan. Add hamburger and onion and fry until brown. Add celery and cook until celery is done. Then add cooked rice and strained tomatoes. Add kidney beans last with salt and pepper to taste. Pour in baking dish and bake about 20 minutes.

Most Lutheran Church Basement Women don't serve Hungarian Goulash because it calls for a mix of celery and kidney beans and things that just don't go together well. It would be like mixing a regular Lutheran with a Wisconsin Synod German Lutheran.

Everyday Jell-O

1 small box Jell-O
1 cup hot water
1 cup cold water

Dissolve Jell-O in hot water. Add cold water and set. This recipe can be doubled.

Most Lutheran Women would add 1 large banana and/or whipping cream for a Mission Festival. But then, some don't. Good for those with new dentures or those on special liquid diets.

Mexican Goulash

1 box spaghetti or noodles
1 lb. bacon
1 can corn
1 can tomatoes
1 can lima beans
1 can peas

Prepare spaghetti or noodles according to directions on box. Fry the bacon and add it to the spaghetti also adding a little of the drippings. Then add corn, tomatoes, lima beans and peas. Drain the liquid from the beans and peas. Season to taste.

A festive dish to bring if the missionaries are from south of the border, even though most Midwest Lutherans don't care for this dish.

Nut Devil's Food

2⅓ cups sifted flour
3 tsp. baking powder
½ tsp. salt
½ cup shortening
2 cups sugar
4 eggs, separated
2 squares chocolate, melted
1 cup milk
1 tsp. vanilla
1 cup chopped walnuts

Sift flour, baking powder and salt together. Cream shortening thoroughly and add sugar gradually until light and fluffy. Add beaten yolks, mixing thoroughly, then melted chocolate, and beat well. Add sifted dry ingredients, alternately with milk, mixing well after each addition. Add flavoring and nuts. Fold in egg whites, beaten stiff but not dry. Bake at 350 degrees. This makes 3 layers or a 9x12 loaf. Bake the layers for 30 minutes and the loaf for 50.

If you are on a committee for the festival, you won't have enough time to make this.

Oatmeal Cake

2 cups oatmeal
2 cups water, boiling
3 cups brown sugar
1½ cups lard

Pour boiling water over oatmeal. Add sugar and lard.

Combine:

2 cups bread flour
1 tsp. soda
1 tsp. salt
2 tsp. cinnamon
1 tsp. baking powder
1 egg

You may add as many raisins and nuts as you like. Bake in a 10x13 pan at 350 degrees for 45 minutes. Serve with whipped cream.

This is kind of a bother for mission festivals. Mrs. Peder Larson said, "Skip the whipped cream for pot luck tables. It's tasty without it".

Preacher's Hotdish

1 lb. hamburger
2 medium onions or less
2 cups celery
1 can tomato soup
1 can mushroom soup
1¼ cups water
1 tsp. chili powder
Salt and pepper to taste
2 cups chow mein noodles

Brown hamburger, onions and celery in small amount of fat. Add remaining ingredients except noodles. Add noodles and mix well. Sprinkle top with additional noodles before baking. Bake at 350 degrees.

We don't know why this is called a Preacher's Hotdish. Maybe it's because the chow mein noodles add a bit more class.

Rhubarb Sauce

4 cups diced rhubarb
Small amount of water
1 cup brown sugar

Put rhubarb, sugar and water in kettle and cook until tender. This is always a good dessert in the spring and early summer.

If you are busy or don't have time to bake or cook for a mission festival, you always have a jar of rhubarb sauce on hand to bring.

Salmon Hotdish

1 cup shell macaroni
1 tall can salmon
1 (No. 2) can peas
3 hard cooked eggs, diced
½ tsp. salt
⅛ tsp. pepper
½ cup breakfast cereal flakes

Boil macaroni in water, to which ¼ tsp. salt has been added, for 5 minutes. Drain. Mix salmon (flaked), peas, diced eggs, salt, pepper and macaroni. Make a white sauce, using juice from salmon for part of the liquid. Pour over other ingredients and mix well. Top with crushed cereal flakes. Bake at 325 degrees for 30 minutes. Serves 6

A tall can of salmon can get kind of spendy, but if you don't have any meat thawed, then you're up a creek without a paddle and might not have any other choice.

Spice Cake

1½ cups brown sugar
2 eggs
1 tsp. soda (in milk)
1 tsp. ground cinnamon
½ tsp. ground cloves
½ cup butter
1 cup sour milk
1 tsp. baking powder in 2 cups flour

Just before putting in pan, add a tablespoon of vinegar. One-half cup chopped nuts may be added if desired.

Make the usual frosting for this cake. Good in the fall of the year.

String Bean and Carrot Hotdish

2 tbsp. butter
2 tbsp. flour
½ tsp. salt
⅛ tsp. pepper
1 cup milk and vegetable juice
½ cup grated cheese
4 medium carrots, cooked
4 eggs, hard-cooked
2 cups string beans, cooked

In top of double boiler, blend butter, flour, salt and pepper. Add the milk and stir until smooth. Melt the cheese in the hot sauce. Put carrots and eggs, both cut in half lengthwise, in bottom of buttered baking dish. Place string beans around them. Pour cheese sauce over vegetables and bake at 375 degrees for 30 minutes. Serves 4.

A good use for all those string beans that you canned.

Sylte
(Head Cheese)

Clean pig's head thoroughly under running water. Place in cold salt water and boil until tender, about 3 hours. Leave in the liquid until cool. Then remove the meat from the bones. Place a clean cloth in a loaf pan. Cut meat into strips and arrange on cloth, alternating lean and fat meat. The rind of the meat should be placed so it will be on the outside of *sylte* roll. Season meat with salt, pepper and allspice to taste. Roll up cloth as tightly as possible to make *sylte* roll. Wrap string about roll and tie firmly. Place heavy weight on roll and press overnight. The cloth may then be removed and the head cheese will retain its shape. Place rolls in brine for 48 hours before using.

Fit for King Olaf!

Tater-Tot Hotdish

1 lb. hamburger, browned and seasoned with salt, pepper and onion
1 small can peas
1 can cream of mushroom soup
1 can cream of celery soup
1 pkg. frozen tater-tots

Put in layers in small casserole as listed. (When doubling the recipe, use only 3 cans of soup.) Bake at 350 degrees for 30-40 minutes. This will make a large cake pan full. It can be prepared the night before and baked the next day.

A lifesaver for a busy Lutheran woman.

Vegetable Hotdish

1 layer of raw potatoes
1 layer of raw onions
1 layer of raw ground meat (seasoned)
1 layer of cooked rice
1 layer of canned lima beans
1 can tomatoes

Arrange layers of onions, potatoes, meat, rice, lima beans and season each layer as desired with salt and pepper. Pour tomatoes over layers and bake at 350 degrees for 2 hours. Serves 6-8.

This would be a Lutheran classic recipe if the lima beans and tomatoes weren't in it but rather cream of mushroom soup.

BIBLE SCHOOL LUNCH BOX

Lunches, whether for school children or grown-ups, should contain substantial food that will be wholesome, nourishing and appetizing. The Bible School lunch should be a real meal with enough variety to form a balanced diet.

A lunch should be packed in a well-ventilated, sanitary container to protect the food and to keep it compact and odorless on opening. Waxed paper should be used to wrap all food, and covered jelly glasses are excellent to use for baked beans, vegetable salad, applesauce, baked apple or for a pudding. Highly seasoned and rich foods should not be placed in a lunch box. Plain, wholesome food is essential for health.

Milk in some form should be included in the daily Bible School lunch – either plain milk, malted milk, or hot or cold Watkins Cocoa, which may be carried in a pint milk bottle or in a thermos bottle, using a straw for drinking. Milk is highly important because it supplies energy and contains the necessary mineral salts, with Vitamins A, B, C, D and G. Milk contains calcium that quiets the nervous system. Fresh fruit in season is appetizing and healthful.

Hard-cooked eggs, cooked 30 minutes, are as digestible as soft-boiled. Peeled, wrapped in a lettuce or cabbage leaf and waxed paper, they will make an appetizing salad. Cooked vegetables as a salad add a note of interest to a box lunch. Raw carrot sticks or celery sticks made crisp in cold water, dried and wrapped in waxed paper make a tasty accompaniment to a meat sandwich.

SUNDAY SCHOOL PICNICS

Jell-O for a Crowd

4 boxes Jell-O
4 cups hot water
4 cups cold water

Dissolve Jell-O in hot water. Be careful to get everything dissolved. Add cold water and refrigerate. When partially set, carefully slice in 1 good-sized banana or 2 small. This will feed about 30 people.

This recipe was used for the 75th Anniversary of the Trinity Lutheran Church Sunday School Picnic.

Company Casserole

1½ lbs. ground beef
2 medium onions
1 can mushrooms
½ cup stuffed green olives
½ cup grated American cheese
Salt and pepper
1 can mushroom soup
1cup milk, blended with soup
1 box Juniorettes, cooked

Brown ground beef and onions; add mushrooms and olives. Stir in cheese and seasonings, soup and Juniorettes. Mix a few cashews and chow mein noodles in with casserole. Bake at 350 degrees for ½ hour. Remove from oven and sprinkle more noodles and cashews on top. Bake another ½ hour.

Macaroni-Spam Bake

2 cups cooked macaroni
1 small onion
1 small green pepper (optional)
¼ lb. cheese
1 can spam
Pimento (optional)
1½ cups hot milk
½ cup butter
1½ cups bread crumbs
4 egg yolks, beaten
1 can mushroom soup
4 egg whites, beaten

Grind onions, pepper, cheese and spam. Melt butter in milk. Beat yolks of eggs; pour over bread crumbs. Add butter and milk. Fold in stiffly beaten egg whites. Mix gently with ground ingredients and macaroni.

Bake in 9x13 pan. Cut in squares. Pour heated (undiluted) mushroom soup over each square when serving.

Fried Chicken for Sunday School Picnics

Preparation: Go out to the chicken coop and find yourself about 14 old biddies that haven't been keeping up their end of the bargain as far as producing eggs goes. Bring them to the chopping block and axe off their heads. Let them flop around for a while – half dead. Whip them into the kitchen and immerse them in scalding water to loosen the feathers. Next, roll up a newspaper, set it on fire and singe the remaining feathers off. (This is done after you lift them out of the boiling water.) Make sure you don't start anything else on fire!! Take all the innards out, and you're ready to start. (If you are planning to serve these chickens for a Sunday noon Sunday School picnic, it's best you do the preparation on Saturday so you're not rushed.) Sunday morning – early a.m. – wash and cut up the 14 chickens. Wipe them dry, season with a little salt and pepper, dip them in beaten eggs and flour, and fry them in hot lard on top of the stove. After they are done frying, put them in a big roaster and let them finish baking while you are at church. When you get home from church, you can take the drippings and make a little gravy.

Tuna Crunch Salad

1 (No. ½) can solid tuna
4½ tbsp. chopped pickles
1½ tbsp. minced onion
1 cup mayonnaise
Dash of salt, if desired
1½ tbsp. lemon juice
1½ cups shredded cabbage
1 small bag potato chips
(coarsely crushed)

Combine tuna, pickles, onion, mayonnaise, salt and lemon juice. Chill in covered dish until ready to serve. Add cabbage and toss. Just before serving, add half of the crushed potato chips and toss lightly. Heap into shallow lettuce-lined salad bowl and sprinkle with rest of the chips.

Grandma's Favorite Baked Beans

For every cup of beans, use 1 rounded tablespoon of brown sugar and 1 tablespoon molasses. Cover beans well with water and boil until hulls start to loosen. Add salt, sugar and molasses and 1 teaspoon dry mustard. Add bacon and a small onion and bake for at least 2 hours or more. 1 pound of beans = a roaster.

- Selma Nestegard

Potato Salad for 100

Boil up 32 pounds of potatoes. Chill. Add 4 bunches of celery, 4 dozen hard-boiled eggs, 8 green peppers, pickles, salad dressing, salt and pepper to taste. Recipe can be doubled for big crowds.

A Sunday School Picnic MUST!

Real Lemonade

Squeeze lemons
Add lemon pulp
Add sugar to taste
Put in ice cubes and chill.

Dessert

Dixie cups or ice cream cones are standard desserts at Sunday School picnics.

LUTHER LEAGUERS AND WHAT THEY EAT

LUTHER LEAGUERS AND WHAT THEY EAT

BEVERAGES

Red Nectar Drink

Delicious, Refreshing Drink

2 tsp. Watkins Cherry Nectar Syrup
2 tsp. sugar

Blend sugar and syrup in glass of water. Stir the mixture and add an ice cube.

Of course you'd have to make several pitchers of this red nectar drink for a thirsty bunch of Luther Leaguers, especially if there were a lot of boys at the meetings. Churches usually don't have ice cubes, but you can chill the nectar in the refrigerator while the meeting is on.

Ice Cream Soda

3 tbsp. cocoa syrup
Vanilla ice cream
1 tbsp. Watkins Vanilla
Carbonated water (cold) serve with siphon

Place syrup in tall glass. Add ice cream. Fill glass using ½ carbonated water and ½ milk. Stir to blend.

A good treat for Luther Leaguers after they've done some volunteer work. Save for special occasions. It's usually not made for everyday.

Watkins Hot Cocoa

2 cups milk
3 tbsp. Watkins Cocoa
Pinch of salt
2 tbsp. sugar
1 cup boiling water
Whipped cream
Watkins Vanilla

Scald milk in double boiler. Blend Watkins Cocoa, salt, and sugar in saucepan. Slowly stir in boiling water and boil 2 to 3 minutes. Stir cocoa mixture into hot milk. Cover and keep hot over boiling water.

Just before serving, use a rotary beater and whip briskly. Serve in hot cup with a dash of whipped cream or marshmallow.

Again, you'd have to make this in large quantities for Luther Leaguers. A dandy treat after a hayride!

MAIN DISHES

Barbeques

10 lbs. hamburger	Salt and pepper
Tomatoes and tomato soup	

Brown the hamburger. Add tomatoes, tomato soup and spices. Keep warm until you serve them in big buns.

Beanie Wienies

8 frankfurters	1 tsp. salt
2 cups cooked navy beans	¼ tsp. pepper
1 onion, sliced	¼ tsp. mustard
1 can tomato soup	1 tsp. Worcestershire Sauce

Split frankfurters lengthwise and cut each piece in half. Place a layer of cooked beans in buttered casserole, then half of the frankfurters and half the onion. Top with remaining beans, frankfurters and onion. Mix the soup with the salt, pepper, mustard and Worcestershire Sauce and pour over other ingredients. Cover and bake at 375 degrees for 25 minutes.

A wonderful treat after summer ball games.

Chili Con Carne

2 lbs. beef
2 lbs. pork
3 tbsp. lard
1 large onion
1 tbsp. chili powder
1 tsp. salt
2 (No. 2) cans kidney beans
2 (No. 2) cans tomatoes
1 tsp. black pepper

Dice meat; brown in lard. Add the onion, cut in small pieces, and the other ingredients. Cook slowly for 2 hours.

An international dish served by Lutheran Church Basement Women. This was never too spicy for the young who can handle chili powder.

Luther League Hotdish

1 cup boiled macaroni
1½ cups milk, scalded
1 cup soft bread crumbs
1 pimento, chopped
1 tsp. chopped parsley
1 tbsp. chopped onion
1 tsp. salt
⅜ tsp. pepper
⅜ tsp. paprika
1½ cups grated cheese
3 eggs

Pour scalded milk over bread crumbs. Combine with the other ingredients, folding in well-beaten eggs last. Bake in a buttered casserole at 350 degrees for 50 minutes.

Most Luther Leaguers wouldn't fuss if you served them hotdish because they're use to it and learned at a young age not to complain.

DESSERTS

Rice Krispie Bars

¼ cup margarine or butter
1 pkg. (10 oz.) marshmallows
6 cups Rice Krispies

NOTE: Use fresh marshmallows for best results

Melt butter. Add marshmallows and melt. Add Rice Krispies. Press warm mixture in a 9x9x2 pan.

These could be made and ready to serve Luther Leaguers in a wink of the eye.

Brownies

2 squares chocolate
½ cup butter
2 eggs
1 cup sugar
½ cup flour
1 tsp. baking powder
1 tsp. vanilla
1 cup broken walnut meats

Melt together the chocolate and butter. Beat together the eggs, sugar, flour and baking powder and then add to the first mixture. Stir in vanilla and nutmeats. Pour on a buttered paper in shallow pan and bake in moderate oven (300 to 350 degrees) for 20 to 30 minutes. Cut into bars.

Brownies are to Luther Leaguers as apple pie is to America.

ABOUT THE AUTHORS

Janet Letnes Martin grew up in the rural setting of Hillsboro, ND where the words 'Norwegian and Lutheran' were synonymous. That said, it was no surprise she graduated from Augsburg College in Minneapolis, MN and married Neil Martin, a 100% Scandinavian-Lutheran man from Newfolden, Minnesota.

In 1983, Janet wrote and published her first book, *Reiste Til Amerika*, a genealogy/history book of her husband's family. From 1984-1992 Janet co-authored with Allen Todnem to write three bestselling books: Cream and Bread, Second Helpings of Cream and Bread and Lutheran Church Basement Women. In 1996, Janet co-authored and published, Our Beloved Sweden: Food, Faith, Flowers & Festivals with her sister, Ilene Lorenz.

Janet officially teamed up with Suzann Nelson in 1994 to write several books relating to their Norwegian/Lutheran/rural backgrounds. These books include: Cream Peas on Toast, Comfort Food for Norwegian Lutheran Farm Kids and Others: They Glorified Mary, We Glorified Rice; They had Stores, We had Chores; Is It Too Windy Back There, Then?; Uffda, But Those Clip-Ons Hurt, Then; Luther's Small Dictionary, From AAL to Zuzuland; You Know You are a Lutheran If . . .; and Just How Much Scrap Lumber Does a Man Need to Save? Their wildly successful book, Growing Up Lutheran, What Does This Mean?, not only won the Minnesota Book Award for Humor in 1997 but was also the inspiration for the popular smashing musicals: "Church Basement Ladies" and "Church Basement Ladies 2, A Second Helping," and the soon to be released musical, "Away in the Basement."

Janet and Suzann are billed as 'those Lutheran ladies' and have performed their comedy routine from coast to coast. They have sold thousands of their CD entitled, "Those Lutheran Ladies, Live in Medora."

In 2007, Janet 'switched gears' and teamed up with author/artist David W. Cook II to write a fabulous humorous book entitled, Lemonade for the Lawn boy: The Executives' Wives' Cookbook Committee.

In addition Janet has written and published Shirley Holmquist & Aunt Wilma, Whodunit? and Helga Hanson's Hotflash Handbook. Janet has been speaking to churches and organizations for over 20 years. She lives in Hastings, Minnesota where she owns and operates her mail-order business: Scandinavian Marketplace, 218 2nd Street East, Hastings, MN 55033 (800-797-4319) and her web/store: WWW.SCANDINAVIANMARKET.COM. Email her at lutheranladies@aol.com.

She is the mother of three daughters and four granddaughters. Her family members, Jennifer, Steven, Sophia, Ariana and Myana Green, Sarah Martin, and Katrina, Andrew and Nora Benedict are the love of her life. She dearly misses her husband, Neil, who passed away in 2006.

Allen Todnem, son of Krist and Cecelia Kallem Todnem, was born and raised in DeKalb, Illinois. His father immigrated to this country from Norway in 1926. Allen's maternal grandparents immigrated from Norway in the late 1800's and settled near Norway, Illinois. Allen attended Waldorf College, Forest City, Iowa, received his B.A. degree from Augsburg College, Minneapolis, Minnesota, and his M.A. From the University of Northern Iowa, Cedar Falls, Iowa. He taught High School in Hastings, Minnesota until 2001, at which time he retired and broadened his Exterior/Interior painting business. He also continued with his canoe trips to the Boundary Waters Canoe Area Wilderness organizing and participating in over 75 adventures. Norwegian Flat Plane Woodcarving occupies his winter months doing commission work as well as one or two sales a year (see below), while he finds himself in the flower garden during the summer. In 1984 he co-authored a book with Janet Martin entitled Cream and Bread. In 1986, they wrote Second Helpings of Cream and Bread. Allen and his wife, Patty Holmen of Windom, Minnesota, reside in Hastings, Minnesota. They have three grown children, Eric, Dan, and Suzanne, and two grandchildren, Ian and Kaitlyn.

Contact at patodnem@comcast.net for more information.

Carvings by Al Todnem

CREDITS FOR ILLUSTRATIONS

David Anderson Collection, NDIRS, NDSU, Fargo, page 5.

Minnesota Historical Society, families can vegetables, page 27.

Minnesota Historical Society, preparing lutefisk. Photo: *St. Paul Daily News*, page 137.

REORDER FORM
FOR

LUTHERAN CHURCH BASEMENT WOMEN

Name____

Address____

City______________________ State ______________Zip ________

No. of Copies____________@ $14.95 / copy Subtotal __________

Postage & Handling $ 3.95 / Book Rate/copy __________

$ 4.95 / First class / copy __________

(Maximum postage on 4 or more books $10.00) __________

MN residents, add 6.5% Sales Tax __________

TOTAL __________

Send check or money order to:
Scandinavian Marketplace
P.O. Box 274
Hastings, MN 55033
Phone: 1-800-797-4319

Visit us online at: www.scandinavianmarket.com
Email: lutheranladies@aol.com

Call or write to the above address or phone number for a free copy of our catalog.

Order online at: www.scandinavianmarket.com